A New Century in WATERBURY VERMONT

STORIES OF RESILIENCE, GROWTH & COMMUNITY

THE WATERBURY HISTORICAL SOCIETY

Published by The History Press
Charleston, SC
www.historypress.com

Opposite: Courtesy of Gordon Miller.

First published 2022

Manufactured in the United States

ISBN 9781467148023

Library of Congress Control Number: 2021949220

Notice: The information in this book is true and complete to the best of our knowledge. It is offered without guarantee on the part of the author or The History Press. The author and The History Press disclaim all liability in connection with the use of this book.

Dedication

Jack Carter
June 28, 1945–June 21, 2021

In memory of Jack, lovingly known as the Mayor of Stowe Street, who inspired our community to honor our town's rich history while creating a vision for its present and future. Jack was an organizer, leader and creative visionary who always led with his heart and mind wide open. Ever the tireless cheerleader, Jack knew how to stir the pot, in the very best of ways. Thank you, Jack, for your dedication to the many Waterbury organizations you directed and with which you served; thank you for shaping Stowe Street with your retail emporium and for your recognition of the renovation of the Stimson and Graves building as well as the historic train station. We salute you as a most remarkable person and we will forever miss you.

CONTENTS

Contents

PREFACE

There are few sentiments more universal and rational, that which manifests itself in a desire to know the past and especially the history of the persons and places with which we are or have been intimately connected.
—*A.M. Hemingway,* The History of Waterbury, *1882*

When planning began for this book, none of us could have foreseen the long months in quarantine due to the COVID-19 pandemic, talking to each other almost exclusively through computer screens. As the final manuscript is being prepared for press, Waterbury, along with Vermont and the rest of the nation, is forging hopefully into the post-pandemic world.

That is what Waterbury and small rural towns just like it across the country have done for three centuries: adapt and persist. In many ways, the story of Waterbury is hardly unique. Like small towns all across the country, Waterbury's history in the first two decades of the twenty-first century is bookended by tragedy. The town mourned with the rest of the nation in the aftermath of the attacks of September 11, 2001, and we have likewise mourned the loss of nearly 600,000 American lives to COVID-19 as we approach the summer of 2021.

In the intervening years, Waterbury has shared in the economic fragility that continues to plague so many small towns. It has had to do its own reckoning with systemic racism. And the town understands the devastation an extreme weather event can inflict.

Preface

The more things change, the more they stay the same—or so it appears. So what is unique to the Waterbury story of the twenty-first century?

Within the larger narrative of small-town life exists a rich diversity and complexity of experiences, cultures and stories. It is within the particular that we find the unique. The unique story of Waterbury in the twenty-first century is constructed and maintained by how we *tell* that story. Sociologist Robert Wuthnow, in his 2013 study "Small-Town America," wrote, "The town as a social identity is preserved and made real through the symbols that represent it, as through the narratives that blossom around those symbols."

Symbols definitive of and integral to twenty-first-century Waterbury life include dairy farms, a lantern parade, a new municipal complex, Village and Town distinctions, the train station, Tropical Storm Irene, VT State Hospital, craft beer, Not Quite Independence Day and radio station WDEV, among many others. What follows are some of the narratives that have blossomed around these symbols, as told by Waterbury community members themselves.

This book does not pretend to be a history text. While all efforts have been made to ensure factual accuracy, the purpose of this book is first and foremost to preserve and share the perceptions and lived experiences of Waterbury citizens in the twenty-first century. In telling these stories, we celebrate our successes, heal from our tragedies and anticipate the promises of the future.

Cheryl Casey, President, Waterbury Historical Society
Steve Van Esen, Former Member, Board of Directors

The Waterbury Public Library has a selection of Waterbury history and Waterbury-related books on loan. Go to waterburypubliclibrary.com to discover forty-two entries.

ACKNOWLEDGEMENTS

A dedicated team of community members saw the need to capture Waterbury's vital history from 2000 to 2020 in book format. Thank you to the Waterbury Historical Society for supporting this effort. A special thank-you to the following people, who devoted their time, energy and countless hours on Google Drive to help this book take shape.

New Book Committee Members
Laura Parette
Cindy Parks
Stephen T. Van Esen
Jane Willard

Production Assistant
Elena Bilodeau

Editorial Team
Fact checkers—Anne M. Imhoff and Jack Carter
Editor—Jan Gendreau
Proofreader—Carolyn Fox

Finally, thank you to the many members of the Waterbury community who shared their stories of resilience, strength and growth in this book. Your words serve as a testament to the power of people working together.

TIMELINE

Waterbury History Timeline 2021

1763	Charter granted by King George III on June 7.
1783	First white settler, James Marsh, arrives and plants corn. Brings his family a year later. He dies in a tragic drowning in 1788.
1790	First town meeting is held. Ezra Butler elected as first town clerk.
1824	White Meeting House is built. Now the United Church of Christ/Congregational.
1826	Ezra Butler is elected Vermont's eleventh governor.
1832	Dr. Henry Janes is born on January 24.
1833	Waterbury Center Community Church is built.
1841	Antislavery convention is held on July 1 and 2.
1849	Railroad arrives on October 1.
1861–65	250 Waterbury volunteers join the Union forces during the Civil War.
1865	Paul Dillingham is elected Vermont's twenty-ninth governor. He advocates for the Vermont Reform School to be built near present-day Exit 10 ramp.
1869	Free Will Baptist Seminary is completed. It is now known as the Green Mountain Seminary building, a restored housing complex on Hollow Road.
1875	Central Vermont Railroad Station is built.
1882	Village of Waterbury is incorporated.

1888 William Paul Dillingham is elected Vermont's forty-second governor.
1891 First patients arrive at the Vermont State Asylum for the Insane (Vermont State Hospital).
1897 On December 14, Mrs. Mark Lovejoy was the first passenger on the Stowe-Waterbury route of the Mount Mansfield Electric Railroad.
1898 Etta Graves and Mabel Morse are the first graduates of the new Waterbury High School on Stowe Street.
1914 Civil War Veterans monument is unveiled to great fanfare on the lawn of Waterbury High School.
1915 Waterbury's beloved Dr. Henry Janes dies on June 10th. He bequeathed his home, the future Waterbury Public Library.
1917 More than one hundred men join to serve in World War I.
1927 Devastating flood hits town with massive destruction and loss of twenty lives.
1935–38 Two-thousand-plus men of the Civilian Conservation Corps build the massive flood-control dam on the Little River. In 1936, President Franklin D. Roosevelt arrives by train to visit the work progress.
1936 Waterbury Rotary Club is organized.
1941–45 438 men and women serve in various capacities during World War II; 10 make the supreme sacrifice.
1950–53 230 men and women serve in the Korean War. Paul Izor and Lester Keith are combat fatalities.
1953 The nearly century-old massive Waterbury Inn, on the corner of Park Row and Main Street, is destroyed by fire on November 4.
1959 Dascomb "Dac" Rowe, longtime (1926–59) high school principal, educator and coach retires.
1960 Exit 10 on Interstate 89 opens.
1963 The town celebrates the bicentennial of its chapter with eight days of festivities.
1966 The last class of Waterbury High School graduates. Harwood Union High School opens in September.
1966 John Lafayette, class of 1957, is declared MIA in the Vietnam War.
1969 First town manager is hired.
1971 Waterbury Ambulance Association is established.
1977 The village is listed on the National Register of Historic Places.

1982	Rusty Parker, town official and longtime WDEV personality, dies. A year later, the village park is named for him.
1983	Green Mountain Coffee Roasters opens its first roasting facility.
1985	Ben & Jerry's Homemade Inc. builds its first factory and moves its corporate headquarters to town.
1991	Revitalizing Waterbury is formed to save the Stimson and Graves Building from demolition.
1991	Green Mountain Club headquarters is opened.
1993	Hope Davey Memorial Field is dedicated in the Center.
1997	Jeffrey Amestoy becomes the chief justice of the Vermont Supreme Court.
1999	Railroad Station restoration project wins major grant.
2000	Town begins the new century with a population of 4,668.
2003	The Ice Center opens and provides ice for the Harwood Ice Hockey teams.
2006	Restoration of the 1875 CVRR station is completed. Green Mountain Coffee Café and Visitor Center occupies the building.
2009	Village and Town Fire Departments merge.
2011	Tropical Storm Irene causes flooding throughout the Village. State Office Complex and Vermont State Hospital close due to extensive damage. Town offices destroyed. Thousand-plus jobs lost.
2012	ReBuild Waterbury becomes the effort for a long-term recovery program to help homeowners affected by the flooding.
2013	Town celebrates its semiquincentennial (250th) anniversary.
2015	Vermont State Office Complex opens in December after major construction of a new building and restoration of historic structures. Jobs begin to come back.
2016	Town Offices, History Center and Library open in new facilities, including historic restoration of the Janes House.
2018	Green Mountain Coffee is merged with Keurig/Doctor Pepper. Begins moving employment out of town.
2019	Multimillion-dollar reconstruction of Main Street begins.
2020	COVID-19 pandemic slows down vitality and affects everything for most of the year. Town population is 5,153 according to estimated 2020 census.
2021	After twenty-plus years of waiting and delay, reconstruction of Main Street is completed.

PART I

AGRICULTURE

1

DAVIS FAMILY FARM

From an interview with Maureen and Mark Davis by C. Parks

The Davis family operates a small ninety-acre dairy farm with seventy-five head that has been in the family for three generations. The farm is on Kneeland Flats Road, straddling both sides of the road. Mark Davis started working with his father, Maurice, when he was fourteen. Mark and Maureen have been married thirty-two years and work as a team. Their three children (two sons and a daughter) help as needed on the farm.

Like most small dairy farmers, the Davises are struggling financially and approaching a crossroads, which may lead to the heart-wrenching decision to sell their herd. Typically, hard times go in four-year cycles followed by a good year, but currently the Davises are entering their sixth year of challenging economics. There is no longer a local market for dairy products; it is all a global market with the fluid market decreasing 30 to 40 percent over recent decades while the cheese and yogurt markets have increased significantly. The Davis family belong to Dairy Farmers of America. The milk is commingled, so the independent farmers no longer know which products they are contributing to.

Vermont's current culture is less supportive of dairy farming than it was historically, as evidenced by the existence of only two dairy farms in Waterbury. Additionally, the local grange has been disbanded. To find repair parts for their equipment, the dairy farmers must drive two hours. With computers now part of tractors and milking equipment, the farmer is no longer able to make repairs himself. The last time a computerized piece of equipment at the Davis Farm had to be repaired, the repair person had to come from New York State. Most of the neighbors are highly supportive of their farm, but occasionally an odd passerby will complain about the smell of manure and become impatient as the Davis cows cross Kneeland Flats Road twice a day six months of the year for pasturing and milking.

While pragmatic, Maureen and Mark point out the benefits of living and working on a farm: loving the land and the animals, raising their children in a wonderful environment, learning the value of a dollar, independence, dedication, being outdoors and developing a strong work ethic. With cows needing to be milked twice a day 365 days a year and the farm needing care 24/7, they have been on only one family vacation. Going to Burlington is referred to as "going on safari."

The Davises would like a better future for their adult children, so Mark and Maureen are exploring growing hemp as an alternative to dairy farming. The 2018 Federal Farm Bill identified hemp as an agricultural product, making it legal to grow and sell the cannabidiol (CBD) extracted from it. For the past two years, the Davises have grown one and a half to two acres of hemp, respectively, using organic methods. They have a business partner who takes care of the processing and marketing. The crop is harvested in the fall, and the leaves and flowers are dried prior to extracting the CBD oil. The adult children are interested in working on the farm to grow more infusibles, including lavender and mints. Growing hemp would allow the farm to continue operating while also meeting the regulatory definition of a farm for participation in Vermont's Current Use Program.

2

EVERGREEN GARDENS OF VERMONT

Carol MacLeod

Evergreen Gardens, located on Route 100 in Waterbury Center, was first established as Garden World in 1978 by the McCain family. Throughout the years, it went through various iterations and owners until it was purchased by David and Carol Loysen in 1992. The Loysens owned the business for ten years and in that time established it as a viable garden center. They did extensive renovations on the main building, erected the barn and enhanced the outdoor retail space. Their commitment to customer service, excellent products and hard work paved the way for the successful future of this garden center.

Mike and Carol MacLeod purchased Evergreen Gardens of Vermont in January 2002. Over the last nineteen years, they have expanded and upgraded the property to turn it into a full-service garden center, including landscaping and design services. They upgraded from one greenhouse and three hoop houses to seven greenhouses for growing and retailing. This coupled with the expansion of the nursery and perennial yards enabled them to grow and offer a wider selection of products. They began growing organic vegetables and herb starts in 2010. Integrated Pest Management (IPM) was introduced in all the greenhouses in 2021; this method uses beneficial insects and other techniques to eliminate the use of environmentally harmful pesticides. Their commitment to responsible environmental practices continued with the installation of four tracker solar panels in 2011 to reduce their carbon footprint. These tracker panels produce all the electricity used by the garden center.

The MacLeods' commitment to customer service and the wellbeing of their staff are the underpinnings to their success. This dedication has brought them multiple awards. In 2016, they were honored with the Retailer of the Year award by the Vermont Nursery and Landscape Association. Additionally, they have a strong commitment to community and schools as an integral part of their business. Evergreen Gardens partners with local schools and educational organizations to support fundraising initiatives. They also partner with the Town of Waterbury and Revitalizing Waterbury to enhance the natural beauty of the area. Education is another component of their commitment to customer service. Evergreen Gardens partners with the University of Vermont in research on the benefits of pollinator gardens and their ability to attract beneficial insects and bees. Educational talks are given at the Waterbury Public Library, garden festivals and on site at Evergreen Gardens. Experts in various fields are brought in to participate and speak at events. Their dedication to their industry goes beyond local involvement. They are members of local and national industry groups, and the owners have served on the board of directors of these groups.

Proud to be an integral part of vibrant Waterbury, Evergreen Gardens of Vermont's commitment to community will always remain strong. Dedication to customer service, excellent products and the wellbeing of the staff will continue to allow Evergreen to develop meaningful partnerships within the Waterbury community.

3

GREEN MOUNTAIN GARLIC FARM

Cindy Maynard

When we first moved to Waterbury, Vermont, in 1979, we had no idea how important organic garlic would become in our lives. We started and successfully operated two adventure travel companies and for twenty-five years we ran bicycle and walking tour adventures throughout the world. We joked with our guests, "We organize and run trips so we can eat fabulous foods from around the globe."

When not on the road, our love of local food and belief that organic and unprocessed food is the key to healthy living led us to become enthusiastic backyard gardeners, producing and storing as much of our own food as possible.

Bob and Cindy Maynard, co-owners of Green Mountain Garlic Farm, in front of the many unique varieties of garlic grown on their Kneeland Flats property in Waterbury. *Courtesy of Cindy Maynard.*

Little did we know that the idyllic place we chose to start our lives together thirty years earlier would become a national leader in the local food movement (localvore). And we would turn our passion for organic, local food into a small Vermont business.

In 2009, when our youngest of three children left for college, we converted an old hayfield, on Kneeland Flats in Waterbury Center, into an organic garlic farm. For several years we grew garlic to develop our own seed stock. We now grow five different varieties of garlic and sell most of it online as seed stock. The garlic is shipped to gardeners and small farms all over the country. The smaller bulbs are used as food stock, and they are sold mostly at our farm stand. With the demand for local food, we also grow and sell organic vegetables, herbs and garlic products. Growing organic, healthy food for our family, friends and neighbors has been one of the most gratifying things we have ever done.

4

MURRAY HILL TREE FARM

Jane Murray

The year after Dr. Bob and Carlie Murray got married, they bought a sixty-acre tract of land in Waterbury Center, Vermont. Carlie, who was raised on a local dairy farm, and Bob, who grew up surrounded by farms and vineyards in California, had hopes of building a produce farm of their own. But when the Vermont Agency of Agriculture examined the land, it determined the Murray farm's clay soil could really only grow two things: berries—which can be labor intensive—and Christmas trees. So, in 1976, they opted for the "easy" option.

At the time, Dr. Bob worked long hours as the only family physician in town. But for decades, he spent all his spare nights, weekends and holidays mowing, weeding, shearing and tending to the trees. Motherhood kept Carlie, a registered nurse, even busier than Bob. But by the time their third child was born in 1984, the first few hundred Christmas trees they had planted were ready to sell.

Their first year in business, trees sold for five dollars each—about the same price Dr. Bob says he charged for an office visit at the time. It took about a decade for the farm to make its first profit, and even that required selling wholesale to a tree lot. But for every tree they sold, Dr. Bob planted two or three more, until eventually Murray Hill Farm was growing nearly twenty thousand Christmas trees on fifteen of its eighty-six acres. (At some point—no one really remembers how or when—the property expanded to eighty-six acres, including fifty acres of forestry the Murrays manage on behalf of the state.) They've had offers from wholesale distributors across the country over the years, but for the Murrays, clear cutting all of the fields never felt right.

The beauty of running a choose-and-cut Christmas tree farm, they had learned, was witnessing the generations of families—many of them neighbors or colleagues at the hospital—who came to find their perfect tree, sled on the hilly farm, snowshoe through the woods, warm up with hot cocoa or mulled cider on the porch, take family photos and eventually return year after year to continue their Christmas tradition. Familiar faces at the farm soon became friends; people who first visited Murray Hill Farm as kids eventually began bringing their own kids to the tree farm to make new family memories. It wasn't just customers who felt called back to the farm every holiday season. On Christmas Day 2019—forty-five years after Dr. Bob and Carlie planted those first trees—their youngest child, Rob, moved back to the farm with his wife, Jane, and their two young boys. Christmas at Murray Hill Farm might look a bit different in 2021 for a multitude of reasons. But together, the Murrays—now technically a third-generation tree farm—look forward to welcoming new and returning customers for a bit of holiday magic for many more years to come.

5

OWL'S HEAD ORCHARD

Jody Bouchard

When I arrived at 2848 Perry Hill Road in Waterbury in 1976, I discovered the remains of an old orchard that had also been a pasture for the Ayers Farm. The Ayers lost all of their cows one night in the mid-1940s, and as a result abandoned the property. Over the next thirty to thirty-five years, the fields turned into woods. The new tree growth choked out the shorter apple trees, ending up killing most of the original trees.

My next-door neighbor, Mitchell Casey, had commented that he would like to put in a sixty-tree orchard on his property so that he could keep his five active sons busy by tending it. That year I received $1,200 back on my taxes, so my daughter and I decided to help Mitchell actualize his dream of having an orchard. The trees I ordered arrived in a huge waxed box as bare roots. When I delivered them to Mitch, I found out that he had changed his mind and wanted only a dozen. That left me returning home with forty-eight trees. Not wanting to waste the trees, I decided to plant them. I discovered that clearing the land and planting the roots was something I actually enjoyed doing. After I got the first forty-eight planted, I bought another one hundred trees.

A large percentage of the trees in the orchard are nameless—experiments with the Agriculture Departments at Dartmouth and the University of Vermont. The ongoing experiment's goal is to produce fruit without the use of chemicals. The orchard is a "no spray" orchard that uses natural predators to control insects. Frog eggs from neighboring beaver ponds are collected and placed in the pond that is located in the middle of the orchard. Minnow traps gather the larvae of dragonflies and are also placed in the pond. The tree frogs get 90 percent of the bugs, so the dragonflies have to really work to find food. It is wonderful to see the dragonflies' variety of colors!

In 2006, my grandson Mason attempted to open the orchard as a U-Pick business. There were too many challenges and the orchard's health was being compromised so we stopped that business adventure option.

I was fortunate to acquire a forty-gallon steam pot and a stainless-steel pulper. This equipment allowed Mason to start his applesauce business. The highlight for Mason was the year that Central Vermont Medical Center (CVMC) purchased his sauce in jars. A year later, CVMC said that it wanted the sauce in one-cup plastic containers. However, all applesauce produced at the orchard is processed in glass jars for easier recycling. Mason decided CVMC didn't meet his environmental goal and backed out of that business venture.

Currently, Owl Head Orchard is open all year long for purchase of the best applesauce on the market today.

For the years that my grandkids were in primary school, their applesauce was being served in the school breakfast and lunch programs. The school bused all the classes up to our orchard so that the students could experience apple picking and working the cider press.

In an effort to keep the orchard running and for me to be able to hand it over to my grandkids, we started a Community Shared Agriculture (CSA) program. Over the past two years, we have doubled our membership.

6

WALLACE FARM STORIES

Rosina Wallace

The Wallace farm, located on Blush Hill in Waterbury, was purchased in 1866 by Sidney and Lavinia Wallace. For years, the farm allowed the family to be self-sufficient. Rosina Wallace's grandparents James and Florence had seven children in nine years. Sadly, James Wallace died in 1918 as a result of the Spanish flu pandemic. Due to Florence's business sense, she, with the help of her children and neighbors, was able to run the farm. By the 1920s, the Wallace family had, in addition to their dairy production, pear, apple and plum orchards along with a maple operation. The family also kept bees and sold honey. Keith, Rosina's father, the son of James and Florence, eventually took over the farm. Working as a farmer, Keith also served as a state representative and as president of the Vermont Farm Bureau. A Keith Wallace Service Award is given to a member of the Waterbury community at Town Meeting each year.

Rosina, a fifth-generation Wallace, was in her twelfth year of teaching and completing a master's degree in health education in 1980 when she decided that teaching was not what she wished to do. Rosina's dad, Keith, asked her if she wanted to farm. She "stepped up to the plate" and moved home to manage the farm until 2018. Rosina milked eighteen to twenty Jersey cows twice a day and tended to the remaining tasks of a dairy farm. Rosina's brother Wally returned to the farm in 1984 to provide help with haying and other specialty projects.

Wallace barn and residence destroyed by fire on Easter Sunday, April 1, 2018. *Courtesy of Gordon Miller.*

Rosina has always been committed to offering the farm experience to children. Farmer Rosina delighted in inviting prekindergarten and daycare-age children on a field trip to the farm every spring, where the children enjoyed hands-on experience petting and even milking a cow. They were treated to samples of cheese and yogurt. A class at the Thatcher Brook Primary School chose Rosina's farm as "One of the 7 Wonders of Waterbury." Rosina also entered the July Fourth parade each year by leading a calf along the parade route. She and a calf were also present at the town's annual Kids Fest celebration. In the summertime, she hosted a picnic for the Fresh Air kids who were staying with local families. In 2008, Rosina adopted Bodhi, a border collie that was her constant companion and protector until Bodhi passed away in 2021.

Tragically, on April 1, 2018, while Rosina was enjoying Easter dinner with a neighbor, the barn caught fire—it was a near-total loss. Initially, Rosina shared that it was the demise of her beloved Jersey cows that was most devastating. As she began the task of digging through the ashes, she grieved the loss of five generations of footprints in the barn that told the story of how farming evolved over the years.

The Waterbury community immediately responded to Rosina and Wally. A You Caring Fund account was set up, resulting in a significant sum of

Sibling co-owners of the Wallace farm are Kay Wallace, pictured at the far right, and his sister, Rosinna Wallace, fourth on the left. They are surrounded by supportive neighbors. *Courtesy of Gordon Miller.*

money. Several fundraising events followed: the Waterbury and Waterbury Center Fire Departments hosted a spaghetti dinner, Stowe Street Café offered a special meal, there was a community talent show, a Country Club of Vermont dinner and dance was held and the local schoolchildren collected pennies and made cards. Rosina proudly shared that when the schoolkids showed their support it was determined that every student had remembered visiting the farm. When the clean-up and rebuilding process began, once again the community helped. Many of the furnishings for their modest home originated from free items posted on the local Front Porch Forum website. The Wesley United Methodist Church provided space for donations of clothing and other miscellany. A group of talented and generous people built the first barn. The community's response to the Wallaces' tragedy exemplifies "community at its best."

While the dairy farm no longer existed, it was vital for the Wallaces to continue to own their 226 acres, which includes 90 acres of open pasture and field and woodland, in order to afford the taxes. They enrolled in the State of Vermont's Current Use Program, a condition of which is that the land must be used for an agricultural purpose. To meet that requirement, Rosina cares for two alpacas and two bovines she has raised from bull calves. They are regularly visited by kids. Additionally, this spectacular and treasured piece of property is enjoyed by a Bible study group, which meets under a tent.

Fortunately, the Wallace legacy will continue, as Wally and Rosina's niece Jenn Dufresne Brett and her spouse, Harold Brett, have interest in being the next generation to farm the land.

7

WOODARD FARM

George Woodard

Heading up Loomis Hill from Waterbury Center, the Woodard Farm comes into full view. The farm is a small hillside property that has been there for years with its white house, gray weathered barns and sheds and old fence posts lining the road. The farm was bought by Walter Woodard in 1912, and it is here he and his wife, Eva, raised their five children. Their son George and his wife, Teresa, bought the farm from his parents in 1947 following World War II, and it became their home along with their four children. In 1961, George sold the farm's cows to Robert Kellett, who was farming at that time on Barnes Hill, near the Water Works Road. George then became a heavy equipment operator on Vermont's newly evolving interstate, and Teresa became a switchboard operator at the Vermont State Hospital. For several years, Jack Sweet, a neighbor, kept heifers in the pastures and hayed the fields, keeping the pastures open.

After the cows left, some of the farmland George and Teresa owned was sold due to increasing taxes and the 1960s trend of selling off land for building lots. The one parcel of land that Teresa Woodard would not agree to sell was the piece with the white farmhouse and the weathered barns. This is where their children were raised.

Their oldest child, Bernard, joined the Air Force, after which he became a carpenter and a machine designer for the automotive industry. Their daughter Joanna went to Washington, D.C., to work for Senator George Aiken. With his mother's suggestion, George Jr. decided to resurrect the

George Woodard, dairy farmer, pictured in his cow pasture on Loomis Hill in Waterbury Center. *Courtesy of Gordon Miller.*

farm and again start milking cows. This was a major commitment, as there had been no cows in the barn for years and frost heaves had taken their toll on the barn's foundation. In 1975, older brother Bernard came back to help out as the barn was jacked up and a new foundation put underneath. With the 1926 Lane tractor sawmill bought in 1973, logs from the farm were milled. The shed was built and the barn repaired just in time for the cows to start milking. They began shipping milk to Cabot Creamery on December 2, 1975. In 1982, George and Teresa's youngest child, Steve, became a veterinarian, returning to Waterbury Center to establish a highly regarded practice. Steve was an important participant in the Woodard Farm's success and the 1990s organic dairy movement. Throughout the years, many high school students worked at the Woodard Farm, experiencing the hard work and commitment needed to run a small farm.

Still, there's so much more to this hillside farm than cows grazing in the pasture and the haying of fields. Sometimes music was heard coming from the old farmhouse in rehearsal for an upcoming Vermont tour of the highly anticipated *Ground Hog Opry*. The reason: in addition to being a farmer, George Jr. is a well-known and well-loved musician, filmmaker and comedian. During the summer, the barn houses the hay for winter, but it's also often where plays are rehearsed. Classic American plays are then performed in small towns throughout Vermont. The hay barn has been used for movie sets such as a diner and a farm machinery repair shop in the black-and-white movie *The Summer of Walter Hacks*, which was set in 1952. The old-style silent movie *The Bad Robbers* was also filmed in the farm's surrounding fields, while the woods were the setting for a Belgium farmstead in the 1944 World War II–era *The Farm Boy*. Throughout the years, the farm setting has been featured in numerous other movies; however, as of this writing, the cows are milked every day and the fields are plowed each summer.

PART II

ARTS AND CULTURE

1

AXEL'S FRAME SHOP & GALLERY

Whitney Aldrich

Named after its founder, Axel Stohlberg, Axel's Frame Shop & Gallery has been in business since 1983, and while it has had several locations in Waterbury, 5 Stowe Street has been its home for over twenty years. In 2013, Axel Stohlberg retired and passed the torch to Whitney Aldrich, a Waterbury resident looking to provide an opportunity for area artists and artisans to showcase their work and gain exposure in the area. Without any framing experience, Whitney dove in and has dedicated half of the space to visual and performing arts in an effort to connect the community with contemporary art, all while learning the deep skill of custom picture framing. Receptions, performances, pop-ups and more are held within the space for free and are open to the public. A popular summertime event, prior to the COVID-19 pandemic, was Music in the Alley, a collaboration between Axel's and TURNmusic, a local contemporary chamber music group. During these events, the strange, obscure service alley of Axel's was transformed into a free, magical musical venue for the community to hear the unique and rich talents of our area musicians.

Whitney hopes Waterbury continues to be a place where art is celebrated and encouraged. Engaging our community through public art is high on her priority list. And perhaps an artist-in-residence program will be on the horizon.

2

GRANGE HALL CULTURAL CENTER

Monica Callan

Located at 317 Howard Avenue, on the green in Waterbury Center, the Grange Hall has operated as a central social and cultural hub for the Waterbury community from its inception in the 1850s as a Baptist church. In 2016, it became the Grange Hall Cultural Center (GHCC) under the direction of new owners, artists Monica Callan and Peter Holm.

The establishment of the GHCC had been long awaited, with Monica involved in efforts to initiate an arts center in Waterbury throughout the years. Numerous attempts were made, though none came to fruition, and with each attempt public engagement grew. Following the local devastation caused by Tropical Storm Irene in 2011, Monica participated in a long-term recovery project guided by FEMA. She advocated for the arts to enrich the rebirth of the town's economic and social viability. Options for an arts center were considered. With the help of many townspeople, Monica created a proposal for a community art center as a critical cog in the wheel of recovery and ongoing economic sustainability. Advocating for the arts as a present and necessary component of daily life is still ongoing, but the language from the feasibility grant they wrote was incorporated into Waterbury's 5-Year Municipal Plan.

To this end, several buildings in the downtown were investigated, numerous people were consulted, partnerships were posited, surveys were taken, feasibility grants were written and people gathered to see what else could be done. But no concrete solution was found until the solution presented itself.

Unknown to most, the leaders of the Grange Hall No. 237 in Waterbury Center were planning to shut their doors and dissolve their chapter. The Grange members approached Monica and Peter, and together they decided to keep the building in public use under new ownership. In February 2016, the building changed hands, and Monica and Peter, along with many people in the community, have been bringing it up to date ever since. Sometimes the best solutions don't happen when or how you think they will.

The Grange Hall Cultural Center continues the building's practice as a community gathering place, with a focus on presenting theater, dance, music, film, arts exhibitions, lectures and arts collaboration and education. It hosts local music, film screenings and film shoots, art jams, dance events, open mics and jazzyoake, poetry readings, crafting sessions and educational opportunities. A rotating schedule of wellness arts and therapies occurs throughout the year, including yoga, Tai Chi, Pilates, Zumba, 5 Rhythms, Reiki/massage, children's kinetic learning and a variety of different dance classes. It is also available for meetings, performances and community or family celebrations. One of its yearly signature events is the Irish Arts Festival that occurs around St. Patrick's Day.

Grange Hall Cultural Center is also home to Across Roads Center for the Arts and GHCC's resident company, MOXIE Productions. Across Roads Center for the Arts is a multidisciplinary, nonprofit arts organization dedicated to opportunities to connect, present and educate through creative activity. It is committed to expanding and celebrating arts across disciplines, cultures, generations, abilities, boundaries and throughout our region. The organization maintains a roster of regular programming offering arts classes, lectures and activities and several art exhibits throughout the year. Each year, two monetary awards are given away to support youth in the arts. The Mitch Siegel Emerging Artist Award grants monies to a graduating high school senior pursuing the arts beyond Harwood Union High School. The Janet DiBlasi Creative Curriculum Award is given to a teacher or team of teachers at Thatcher Brook Primary School or Crossett Brook

One of the MOXIE Productions being performed in Grange Hall Cultural Center. *MOXIE Productions.*

Middle School who use the arts as a component of curriculum learning, connecting core standards with meaningful art applications.

MOXIE Productions is dedicated to the presentation, education, development and celebration of diverse, collaborative, innovative and accessible community building theater and art. MOXIE Productions made theater in Vermont and New York City prior to its formal establishment in 2001. It provides ongoing support of new work and fosters writers through their readers' theater cabarets, guest artist workshops, writers' groups, the One & Only Series (solo performance) and the Vermont Contemporary Playwrights Forum grants. This program presents playwrights with a comprehensive development process followed by a complete production of their work and support thereafter. MOXIE Productions offers an artist-in-residence program, providing a laboratory space for new work to emerge with artists working with collaborators or individually. In a retreat-like setting, artists can focus fully on their projects to actuate their visions. Time and studio space are available, as well as the support of a production team to help them present their work to Grange Hall Cultural Center audiences at the completion of their residencies. Ongoing support to bring their creations to new audiences follows.

3

JEREMY AYERS POTTERY

Jeremy Ayers

Driving down Elm Street in Waterbury, it is hard to miss the sign for Jeremy Ayers's pottery workshop and small studio. On any given weekday, and often on weekends, this forty-something artist and craftsman can be found with dirty clay-covered hands shaping a bowl as his kiln emanates heat. He often has a helper who is lining up the next load for the kiln or shaping clay handles for the next batch of mugs. As he wipes the clay off his hands, he will show you the small area where completed bowls and mugs and vases are on display.

Jeremy and his wife, Georgia, and their two young sons live at the unique, historical and long-standing address of 18 Elm Street in Waterbury. He is the fifth-generation Ayers to be associated with this three-quarter-acre property at the edge of both the commercial district and the residential district of this town—and Jeremy is proud of this. He owns the property equally with his cousin Ben Ayers, who lives above the studio area. An aunt, Betsy Ayers Shapiro, lives in an apartment on the property. It is a family thing.

There is much history in this small area. The original house, carriage barn and icehouse were built in the 1880s by Orlo Ayers, Jeremy's great-great-grandfather, who was born in 1857 in the Ricker Mountain area and died on this property in December 1936. Orlo was a wheelwright who, with a few other workers, made and repaired carriages and sleighs in the barn where the pottery studio now exists. By the turn of the twentieth century, Orlo had left the wheel business and established a hardware store across

Jeremy Ayers turning pottery at his pottery studio located at 18 Elm Street in downtown Waterbury. *Courtesy of Dylan Griffin.*

Elm Street and near Main Street at the site of the current Craft Beer Cellar. He bought the building from a brother-in-law who had gone out of business there as a blacksmith. The hardware store was a success, and Orlo became a town father of Waterbury.

In 1890, Orlo sold the house and small barn and moved them from the corner site to other locations on Randall Street. Jeremy's grandfather told the story that Orlo and his wife, Bessie, slept in the house as it rested on logs, halfway on its journey to its new site. The current building, 18 Elm Street, and the large barn behind it, were completed in 1892. The new house was connected to the new barn, where the outhouse for the site was located. In this barn, Orlo established a "gentleman's farm," where he kept a couple of cows, chickens and a horse. A couple of hooks that kept an animal in its place still hang on the walls.

Orlo's son Max, born at 18 Elm Street in 1890, graduated from Norwich University in 1914 with a degree in engineering. Before he was thirty, Max gradually took over the hardware business from his aging father. Under Max's supervision, the carriage barn became a storage area for the store. It was expanded to add a four-car garage at ground level and more storage on the second floor in 1927 before the flood. The cattle area became a place for more storage, and the outhouse was removed—replaced, as family legend would have it, by the first flush toilet in Waterbury. Soon after the flood reconstruction, Orlo rented rooms upstairs. Orlo and Bessie both died by the end of 1936. Max turned the family home into apartments. He managed the hardware and plumbing business until he turned sixty-five, when it was dissolved. He lived twenty-five more years.

By the mid-1980s, the house had fallen into disrepair, and much work needed to be done to restore it to its earlier glory. Jeremy's grandparents Gleason and Marion Ayers were up to the task and retired to 18 Elm Street. Over the next ten years, they planned well and worked hard to make it a comfortable and efficient home for themselves and visiting family members. Jeremy remembers visiting his grandparents at their house in Waterbury. He and his family visited often. Thanksgiving there became a family tradition and included the entire family and visitors, too.

Jeremy's dad, Bob Ayers, born in the 1940s, grew up in this area of Waterbury and passed this house every day of his twelve years of walking to school. Because the house was at this time rental property, Bob did not develop any ties to this part of his family story. Bob was close to his parents but not so close to the history of 18 Elm. It was different for Jeremy.

Jeremy visited his grandparents in this house often, and this was the beginning of a closeness to his grandparents as well as the Waterbury property. In Jeremy's words, "Visiting my grandparents in this house was, for me, like stepping into a different decade entirely. The qualities of the century-old home that were intact mixed with the style in which my grandparents lived….I always felt like I was stepping into a 1950s time capsule. My grandparents were in good health into the 2000s, and this is when my wife, Georgia, and I truly enter the 18 Elm story."

Jeremy's love for this family place evolved when he started to spend time with his grandparents for several hours one day each week. At first, his grandfather was quite doubtful of an artist's ability to be of any help. But gradually, week by week, month by month, Jeremy demonstrated his skill at getting the tasks done. Sometimes his grandfather would show him once how a certain task was to be done, and Jeremy showed that he could master the skill to his grandfather's satisfaction.

Gradually, Jeremy's grandparents began to depend on him and trust him. The bonds strengthened. By 2008 or so, Jeremy and Georgia had started thinking about a family for themselves. They gave up their home in Lamoille County and moved into an apartment at 18 Elm Street. Gleason and Marion began to depend on Jeremy and Georgia more and more. In their late eighties, health concerns became an issue. The trust level of the grandparents increased as they discovered the capabilities of their grandson and his wife. Jeremy was trusted so completely that he assumed the finances and the care of the house and property.

In 2010, Jeremy decided that his roots needed to be established in Waterbury at 18 Elm: he needed to be where Orlo took a leap of faith in establishing his carriage business and where Max became an entrepreneur with a successful hardware store. He needed to keep the home and barns of his ancestors that had been refurbished by Gleason in the family, and he wanted his children to grow up in this small town as Bob, his father, did. Jeremy's roots began in the cellar of the 18 Elm Street house, where, in 2010, he set up his potter's wheel and kiln. He improved the lighting in that basement as well as the electrical circuit, ordered a mass of clay, sat at his wheel and began Jeremy Ayers Pottery in Waterbury, Vermont.

Much has happened at 18 Elm since the first mug was pulled out of the kiln and set to cool in 2010:

- both of Jeremy's grandparents died, his grandmother in 2010 and his grandfather in late 2011;
- Jeremy and Georgia and nine-month-old Fletcher walked Gleason out of Tropical Storm Irene floodwaters on August 28, 2011;
- Jeremy lost all of his basement pottery equipment in the same flood, Tropical Storm Irene;
- Jeremy took over responsibility for the post-flood recovery and rebuilding of the family house for the next six months;
- Jeremy's father and his siblings opted to use their inherited funds to restore and renovate Orlo's entire carriage barn into apartments and a studio for new pottery equipment;
- Jeremy Ayers and his cousin Ben Ayers assumed ownership of 18 Elm in June 2019.

Today, Waterbury is a lively and successful small Vermont town. It is a place that one wants to visit. There is much to attract Vermonters and folks from the forty-nine other states—fine restaurants, unique breweries, interesting houses and buildings, access to skiing and snowboarding and 18 Elm—home of Jeremy Ayers Pottery.

4

MAKERSPHERE

Fostering Creativity in Our Community

MK Monley

In 2012, as part of the recovery from Tropical Storm Irene, FEMA held a community-wide meeting focused on imagining a new future. At the meeting, several individuals voiced high hopes and imagined an art center and a community steeped in the creative economy. The represented groups, inclusive of recreation, economics and tourism, each expressed enthusiasm for an art center as part of our immediate recovery from the flood, as well as a long-term vision for an art center at our community's core.

Building on this initiative, in 2015 a group of artists and maker enthusiasts met to envision creating a physical space for artists and makers to work and strengthen the town's creative economy while sharing their pieces with the community. Led by Whitney Aldrich of Axel's Frame Shop & Gallery, community members came together to build support for this idea.

A community-wide survey seeking feedback and ideas was one of the group's initial steps. Additionally, the team explored models for successful community maker projects in Vermont and elsewhere. The group immediately recognized there was a lack of access to creation spaces within the town. Local educators noted that high school students were graduating without experience in wood shop, metal shop and home economics. In early conversations with community members, and backed by survey results, the group committed to the concept of maker spaces to ensure that people within the community learn and practice skills to support self-sufficiency—a fundamental mainstay of the independent Vermont way of life. A maker space (fostering a host of opportunities for learning and creating), rather than an art center, evolved as the primary focus of the group.

A priority was to have a maker space hub in the downtown area, walkable for schoolchildren and visible for visitors and locals. A founding member of the group, Mame McKee, offered Seminary Arts, a ceramic and art studio in Waterbury Center, as a satellite site. Mame had been working in the creative sector for decades; this partnered well with the maker concept. In 2017, a Mini Maker Faire was held as part of Waterbury Arts Fest, further introducing the community to the model. It was a major success. In September 2018, Waterbury Area MakerSphere Cooperative Inc. became a 501c3. The founding board included John Bauer, president; Mame McKee, vice president; Don Schneider, treasurer; MK Monley, secretary; and members at large Whitney Aldrich, Sarah-Lee Terrat, Marianne Corcoran, Brian Schwartz, Bob Paolini, David McPhee, Tabbatha Henry, Wade Hodge and Liz Schlegel.

At this time, the owners of Factotum, an apparel printing business in Waterbury, held an open house at their newly purchased property in the heart of downtown, at 30 Foundry Street. Members of MakerSphere attended and discussed their ongoing search for a local maker space with the owners of Factotum, Cris and Meeghan Jones. Supportive of the creative arts, Cris and Meeghan offered to rent the upstairs offices at their shop to the MakerSphere group.

While this space did not allow for the "dirty arts" (wood and metal shops), it did lend itself to studio areas for artists and other creatives (writers, video and audio producers) with additional space for classes and meetings. In March 2019, MakerSphere signed a lease to rent the upstairs of 30 Foundry. Half of the offices welcomed artists and creatives while the other half was dedicated to offices for individuals and coworking space.

The year 2019 brought exciting community collaborations for MakerSphere: the Waterbury Arts Fest; the NQID Parade; workshops for making clay tiles, wooden ornaments and lanterns for the River of Light parade; collaboration with the Waterbury Land Initiative to sponsor a Shutesville Hill Wildlife Corridor photo contest; the Waterbury Winterfest Art Walk with studio tours; and the making of Love Bombs as a public art project. MakerSphere continued its creative energy until February 2020, with artists' gallery shows at 30 Foundry Street, woodcarving workshops, clay classes and painting classes.

All this changed in March 2020 with the arrival of COVID-19 and the subsequent shutdown of the community, state and country. Both MS locations were closed, adult programs were canceled and all children's programs were switched to virtual classes.

Still, efforts continued. Following the governor's declaration of a state of emergency, community makers were organized to make reusable fabric masks, with MakerSphere providing all necessary materials. This mask making mission brought together over one hundred makers to sew masks for healthcare providers, essential workers and the local population, including children. The almost three thousand completed masks were provided at no cost to recipients.

In 2021, as of this writing, MakerSphere is slowly and safely reopening on a limited basis, providing individual creative studios, virtual art clubs for children and in-person ceramic memberships. The annual River of Light parade was reimagined and included participation with surrounding communities. Rather than parade participants marching through the town, cars filled with viewers drove from Dac Rowe Field to Crossett Brook Middle School, Waitsfield Elementary School and Red Hen Bakery in Middlesex to witness fields lined with the beautiful lit lanterns crafted by local schoolchildren. The entire Winooski Street bridge was lit, welcoming cars to pass through to the other venues on the route. Always an exciting event, this reimagined approach was extremely successful, bringing a great deal of pride to the creative community and schoolchildren for their impressive efforts during this difficult time.

A relatively new organization, MakerSphere is built on the belief that people in the community are makers who want a place to work with shared tools and equipment. Waterbury Area MakerSphere Cooperative is dedicated to fostering creativity by providing educational opportunities and workspace for all ages. People are encouraged to share their knowledge and build their resourceful skills in the arts, crafts and trades. This has been MakerSpere's guiding model prior to COVID-19 and continues to be a solid vision and motivation. You are invited to join. What will you make?

5

OFFBEAT BRYCE PRODUCTIONS

Bryce Douglass

In 2000, I was only thirteen, but even at that point I had a "lifelong" interest in capturing audio and visual. To that point, the interest included everything from stop-action animation with my matchbox cars when I was six to creating videos for the Harwood Union High School administrators and student body while I was a student and then working to tell individual stories while in the video program at Burlington Tech Center.

In 2011, I received a certificate in documentary filmmaking from Burlington College. I worked as a freelance videographer and editor for public access stations MMCTV and ORCA, produced personal tribute videos and pursued my interest in comedy as "Offbeat Bryce" on YouTube. Additionally, I completed some project-based work for Green Mountain Self-Advocates (GMSA) in Montpelier for their program connected to the UVM Center for Inclusion, followed the River of Light parade and provided a couple of short films based around the development and the parade itself through my independent business, Offbeat Bryce Productions (OBP).

In 2015–16, all this finally led me to the chance to document the creative process of mural artist Sarah-Lee Terrat of YeloDog Design in Waterbury Center for the "new" human services building at the Waterbury State Complex. I documented Sarah-Lee Terrat's research and meticulous creative process that resulted in the beautiful and meaningful twenty-seven-by-fifty-foot mural, inspired by the poetry of a former patient at Waterbury State Hospital. I was particularly pleased to be able to share the story of the poet, Jeanne Killary, and another patient, Merrill Bennet, to shed light on something that is important to me: people are more than the disability we often use to define them. The mural brought the long history of the Waterbury State Hospital to life. I feel that being able to follow the development of the artwork and share my film with the community deepened the connection and appreciation for the artwork in Waterbury.

I am grateful for the understanding of the time and logistics required to follow the mural production shown by Sarah-Lee, the State of Vermont, the architects and the Vermont Council on the Arts. I am particularly grateful to Jeanne Killary's brother, Jim, who spent a great deal of time sharing the story of his younger life with Jeanne and trusting me with the story of her personal struggles in life. The accommodations of all of these people allowed me to produce a piece of film that would not only show the artwork but also tell an important human story.

In 2018, I was fortunate to have Revitalizing Waterbury ask me to document the process of a piece of public art they had selected. *The Waterbury Special* is a metal sculpture created by Phillip Godenschwager of Atlantic Art Glass and Design in Randolph that depicts several historic buildings and forms a train displayed on the side of the railroad bridge as you enter Waterbury village. Interestingly, the engine that heads this train was yet again inspired by Merrill Bennet's many drawings that the Waterbury Historical Society has on display in Dr. Janes House. The artist drew on the beautiful architecture that Waterbury has to offer, and his attention to detail was best shown and appreciated through the film process and video creation. I was able to get much closer to the physical pieces of art so the detail that exists high above Main Street was accessible to the community audience.

I appreciate RW funding this project and Phillip for allowing me into his process. This was difficult for this artist, who better expresses himself through his work than his words, but he was able to let go and trust me to tell the story of his decision making and the painstaking work that went into the completion and installation of this beautiful sculpture.

I am so pleased to have the opportunity to create films that provide a window into the process of public art and increase community interest and connections to these projects. I really enjoy documenting the artistic process to increase community awareness and appreciation of all that goes into public art and the underlying connections those pieces of art have to the broader population. It is a time-consuming process that takes several months of filming and then weeks to months of editing to tell the stories, but I feel the window this gives into the process and the value of these works of art is important to our community and beyond. I hope organizations will continue to provide opportunities for public art to add to the beauty, history and visual interest in Waterbury and beyond. With this, I hope I will be able to create more films documenting those works, sharing the artists, their energy, details of their work and the deeper meanings and connections these works have to our Waterbury community.

As of this writing, I am a thirty-three-year-old native Vermonter. I am fortunate to be part of this community and grateful for the appreciation it has shown for my work.

6

ARTIST SARAH-LEE TERRAT

Sarah-Lee Terrat

I came to Vermont at age twenty-nine from New York City, where I was a freelance artist creating murals and illustration and teaching art. On a visit to Vermont in 1985, I found a tiny print ad in the back of the *Times Argus* newspaper—Ben & Jerry's was searching for a designer with a variety of design experience who could hit the ground running. I applied and interviewed without my full portfolio or interview clothes. Little did I know, I had just what they needed. We clicked, and two weeks later I moved up from the city and worked for twelve years for B&J. It was an exciting time, helping to build a small company into a worldwide brand, and all with a new kind of socially conscious business template.

Eventually, I was drawn to freelancing again. I started YeloDog Design, specializing in murals and fine art installations, as well as illustration, graphic and environmental design. My clients were local and not-so-local businesses and individuals.

The State of Vermont commissioned me to design the 2001 State Quarter as part of the National State Quarter Program. Governor Howard Dean took a flip chart of my rough sketches around the state for months, showing them to people after meetings and speeches to get local opinions on which sketch and subject they preferred. Maple syrup won out. At the coin unveiling ceremony at the statehouse, a promotional video of a farmer tapping trees cleverly morphed into the illustrated Vermont Quarter image. My young son Henry jumped up next to me and yelled, "Look Mom! It's

Pop!" Henry's father, George Woodard, was the third generation to make syrup on his Loomis Hill family farm. Now Henry, grown up, is the fourth generation to carry on the tradition.

In 2015, I applied for an Arts in Public Buildings Grant from the Vermont Arts Council for a mural project in the Vermont State Office Complex, on the site of the former Vermont State Hospital. The hospital and its relationship with Waterbury have always fascinated me. The social history of the Vermont State Hospital and its effect on Waterbury is a delicate and emotional one, and the town has only recently shed its cloak of being "the town they sent you to if you weren't right."

The mural I created for the complex's central lobby tells the interwoven stories of the hospital and its relationship to Waterbury through pictures. It is based on an inspiring poem called "Green and Gold" written by a talented patient at the hospital named Jeanne Killary.

Waterbury has certainly come a long way to reinvent itself, and I'm proud to say that I live here and have been a part of this reinvention. A lively balance of diverse opinions and visions and a great deal of commitment and hard work have forged this transition. Even after a trying blow like Tropical Storm Irene in 2011, Waterbury citizens got back on their feet and helped their neighbors to rebuild. I've never lived in a place where people work together like they do here, and I love being part of it and contributing in ways that can help keep this community vital.

I was a founding board member of Revitalizing Waterbury and a founding board member of Waterbury Area MakerSphere, a cooperative dedicated to fostering creativity in our community by providing educational opportunities and workspace for all ages. We help people share their knowledge and build their creative skills in the arts, crafts and trades.

Murals and Public Artwork in Waterbury

Arvad's | For the first mural, I re-created downtown Waterbury at a particular time in history, during the 1930s when the reservoir dam was being built and Waterbury was host to hundreds of workers from all over the world. Many local people helped by providing me with information and inspiration about the history of Waterbury.

For the second mural, the Arvad's owners Maryann and Jeffery Larkin said, "Do whatever you want! We trust you." Artists don't get offers like that very often. So, I painted a pub scene and I invited Vermonters (including several Waterbury locals) of many eras and backgrounds, all socializing together in a rollicking party. A guide to each character and their significance and accomplishments still exists at the Vermont History Center along with the restored mural presented in framed sections.

The two murals originally painted on site at Arvad's now have new homes in separate locations. The first one (painted in 1999) is in portions at the Waterbury Railroad Station and in the Waterbury town office building. The second mural (painted in 2007, restored 2019) is now permanently installed in the Vermont History Center in Barre.

Waterbury Public Library | Donor Tree Mural for the Waterbury Public Library (painted in 2014), Washington County Crossing Main Street (after Tropical Storm Irene, 2011)

Vermont State Office Complex | *Green & Gold* (mural 2016)

Ben & Jerry's Factory, Route 100 | Design work in the public tour of the facility includes much of Sarah-Lee's environmental and graphic design work from her years at Ben & Jerry's.

Cold Hollow Cider Mill | An illustrated imaginary Vermont family, created by Sarah-Lee and the owners of Cold Hollow, resides throughout the retail and online spaces at the mill.

PART III

BUSINESS

1

JOSEPH ARCHITECTS

Joe Greene

I started Joseph Architects in 2000. Although my professional design experience had been diverse, much of my career experience was focused in the healthcare sector. Given our relationships with hospitals, nursing homes and extended care facilities in Vermont, New Hampshire and Maine, I knew Joseph Architects could be a welcomed resource in central Vermont.

After moving to Waterbury, I joined the Waterbury Planning Commission and the Waterbury Economic Development Committee (WEDC). These were two organizations for which I felt my skills were well suited, helping to influence the future development of Waterbury. My wife and I would be happy raising a family here. As a member of the Planning Commission (for ten years), I was involved in the Town Municipal Plan update. As a group, we recognized the community had many energetic and exciting groups; however, they were all vying for the same limited resources. There was no overarching organization to help manage these groups. The Planning Commission then developed the Waterbury Community Fair, which was held before the Town Meeting to educate voters. The fair brought groups, organizations, residents and municipal bodies together to discuss the community, its interests and vision for its future. This event was a positive community event for several years. As a member of the WEDC (for three years), I was involved in assisting small Waterbury startups gain access to local community development block grants and other funds.

My relationship with Pilgrim Partners, as their collective architect of choice, had a great influence on Joseph Architects over the years. Creating master plans, designing buildings and navigating Vermont's onerous regulatory red tape, our work has been instrumental in the transformation of Pilgrim Park into a professional office, manufacturing and technology park.

Joseph Architects' influence extends beyond Pilgrim Park to Main Street, Stowe Street, Demerit Place, River Road, Route 100, Route 2 and into Duxbury and Moretown.

- Demerit Place: The conversion of the former Freedom Chevrolet auto dealership into 9,500 square feet of office space and the conversion of two 10,000-plus-square-foot storage buildings into office and laboratory space.
- Hannon Home Center, Aubuchon Hardware: 16,000-square-foot home improvement facility and ST Paving: 7,000-square-foot commercial building at the intersection of US Routes 2 and 100.
- The Ice Center: 32,000 square feet. In 2000, I was approached by a passionate group of community members to design a community indoor ice-skating facility. Their tireless efforts allowed them to raise the funds needed to bring the Ice Center of Washington West to fruition. This is a destination for all indoor ice enthusiasts, including visits from the Boston Bruins.
- Route 100 is the home of a new 16,000-plus-square-foot facility, Artisan Coffee, a specialty beverage company that not only manufacturers coffee and tea products but also trains baristas and provides world-class product testing and quality control.
- Our most recent project is the design and permitting of a new 18,000-square-foot retail sporting goods facility with a state-of-the-art indoor firing range for Henry Parro. This project redevelops the western entrance to our community on Route 2.
- We were retained by Perry Hill Partnerships and teamed up with fellow local architect Jennifer Lane to design and permit a new three-story mixed-use office and retail building at the dry bridge on Stowe Street.

Our staff (nine employees strong at its peak) has touched many areas throughout our community, with renovations converting the former Arvad's restaurant into the new McGillicuddy's Pub, renovations to the Best Western

Hotel and the expansion of the original Alchemist on Crossroad. Waterbury Center renovations include the conversion of the 35,000-square-foot former Karl Suss America facility into a world-class research and development facility. Also, we worked with Central Vermont Medical Center to create the Waterbury Express Care at the Bisbee's building on McNeil Road.

I'm proud of our commitment to our community and our environment. As featured in the 2014 *Green Building & Design*, we have several LEED (Leadership in Energy and Environmental Design) Certified projects. Three are in Waterbury.

- 152 South Main: LEED Silver–conversion of an auto dealer and service center into class-A office.
- 150 Pilgrim Park: LEED Gold–80,000-square-foot expansion of mixed-use class-A office and manufacturing facility.
- Waterbury Center Innovation Center: LEED–conversion of 35,000-square-foot manufacturing facility into an inspiring, innovative research and development facility.

Joseph Architects is also a longtime supporter of Waterbury community youth sports: Clyde Whittemore Little League and the Ice Center of Washington West. We've also been very happy to provide assistance to Brookside Primary School for their outdoor playground and treehouse as well as Crossett Brook Middle School, providing assistance with ADA access concerns.

The turn of a century and subsequent turning of decades and moments of natural disasters all create moments of reflection and opportunity. Opportunity to learn from our past and to improve our future. My profession deals with the built environment. It is with that built environment that we may support and influence that future. What I've personally witnessed in the past twenty years as a proud Waterbury resident and business owner is that we have an immensely energetic, passionate and forward-thinking community that truly knows what it's like to ride the highs and the lows. My hope is that we do not become complacent. We must not just stay the course. We *all* must continue to improve the way we steward our community to ensure that our children and their children may also enjoy the benefits of this place we call home.

2

NEW ENGLAND LANDMARK REALTY

Cindy Lyons

Tony Walton and Lynn Taylor started New England Landmark Realty (NELR) in 2007 with a vision: give each client what they need, not just a one-size-fits-all approach. Six months later, they brought on Cindy Lyons as another partner and began to grow the business.

Waterbury has come a long way since we opened in 2007 during a recession. We have not forgotten the people who supported us along the way. We opened our office at 26 North Main Street, next door to the town library and the new municipal offices.

New England Landmark Realty's goal has always been to give back to the community and treat agents professionally. We found this to be an important role to fill. Tony was and still is a mentor; he was on the board of the Children's Early Learning Space. Cindy has been involved with Revitalizing Waterbury for many years, first as a committee chairperson, then as a board member and now as a participant in the Waterbury Area Development Committee. She has also volunteered at the Waterbury Food Shelf. Other NELR agents are working with area seniors and on the boards of nonprofits.

Waterbury has always been close to our hearts. We love working in downtown Waterbury with the ease of popping into the shops and restaurants. The shop owners and restaurant owners/waitstaff are simply wonderful, and they welcome us as we stop by to say hello. Waterbury is synonymous with community.

Main Street reconstruction is a significant facelift to a community in every sense of the word. We plan on being here for a long time because we love Waterbury and all the people who contribute to make it what it is. We always tell prospective home buyers, "If you want a true sense of community, you need to buy in Waterbury."

Throughout the years, New England Landmark Realty has grown to its current size of eighteen professional real estate agents and brokers, and we continue to grow. We are now able to service central and northern Vermont, as well as many counties in between. Still, our true love is for the Waterbury community.

3

PILGRIM PARTNERSHIP AND PILGRIM PARK

Steve Van Esen and Beverley Young

The area northeast of the railroad tracks and behind the railroad station referred to today as Pilgrim Park has served Waterbury in a number of ways since the town was settled in 1793. It was originally a pasture for residents' livestock until the railroad was constructed in 1849. In the early days of the railroad, it was used for cattle pens for holding livestock for shipping and construction of sidings for the railroad. In 1899, the Mt. Mansfield Electric Railroad built a rail line across the area heading toward Colbyville on the way to Stowe. That operation was short-lived and ceased in 1932.

The Pilgrim Plywood Company was incorporated in 1924 with six directors, including Alton G. Wheeler of Waterbury and other members from Richford and Northfield, Vermont, and Woburn, Massachusetts. On the south end of the property, a twenty-thousand-square-foot factory was completed in 1925 to manufacture hardwood plywood. The factory had tripled in size by the time it closed in 1962. Many people worked for Pilgrim Plywood over the years, as many as 150 at one time. The hardwood veneer was used in construction of radios and veneer cores in rubber heels for shoes replacing metal cores. The company owned more than five thousand acres of forestland purchased from the Last Block Company on Ricker Mountain to supply logs for manufacturing in addition to purchasing logs from local farmers. Pilgrim Plywood was closed in 1962 due to competition from cheaper plywood imported from Japan.

Steve Van Esen and Edward Steele proudly display their "Pilgrim" connections as co-owners of Pilgrim Partnership in Waterbury. *Courtesy of Beverley Young.*

In 1956, the A.G. Anderson Concrete facility was built on the site to supply concrete used during construction of I-89. The property was later purchased by the Pilgrim Partnership and incorporated into Pilgrim Park.

The Pilgrim Partnership was formed in 1985 by members Ed Steele, Steve Van Essen, Wendell Parker and Paul Reed. They began acquiring properties around Pilgrim Park, including both the site of Pilgrim Plywood, A.G. Anderson Concrete and other parcels totaling about twenty acres. As they began the design and permitting process for the industrial park known as Pilgrim Park, two of the original four partners remained: Edward Steele and Stephen Van Esen (The Pilgrims). Their vision was to create an industrial park that would grow and be beneficial to their community of Waterbury. Their motto was "Helping Local Business Grow."

This journey started when Steve brought Bob Stiller, founder of Green Mountain Coffee Roasters (GMCR), from his small coffee shop in Waitsfield to 40 Foundry Street in Waterbury. They needed equipment for the roasting process and administrative offices, and it was obvious they'd require more space for growth. In 1991, the first twenty-thousand-square-foot building in the park was built by local contractor Gary Vest.

Preparation for this first building was significant. The former Emery home, across the railroad tracks from Batchelder Street, was removed, and the Pilgrim Plywood building had to come down. To have space to expand the park, S.T. Paving needed to relocate. GMCR purchased the company's building and gave it to the Town of Duxbury to reassemble and use as a town garage. Pilgrim Partners purchased a parcel in Moretown at the corner of Route 2 and Route 100 and built a new home for S.T. Paving. To provide parking for the railroad station and surrounding areas, two historic buildings came down: the Bailey building just behind the station, a seed and grain building; and the Freight House, a lumberyard for many years. Noting the historic value of this structure, the Pilgrims contracted with a local, Amity Baker, to record the historic value and existence of this building; her research and documentation were recorded in a publication, *The Bailey Building*. History lovers hated to see them lost but found consolation in knowing the Freight House was given to a nonprofit in Lincoln, Vermont, and was rebuilt as an arts center playhouse. Also, a new home supply business was built in Moretown next to S.T. Paving.

So, with the land open, the building continued for GMCR, with many additions to the original twenty-thousand-foot structure; one of the most notable was the connection of the huge roasting facility to the adjacent distribution center via a walkway over the road. GMCR was the only tenant in this structure.

Construction of Pilgrim II by local Lee Delphia served as office space for the State of Vermont, Black Diamond Ski Wear, Ivy Computer, Caldera CookTop, Corvel nursing agency and Country Walkers, all local businesses. Pilgrim 5 was designed to look like a Monitor barn by Joseph Greene Architects and was built by Joel Baker. The initial tenants were Canus Soap; Dartmouth Journal Services; Sheryl Stancliffe, massage therapist; and finally a space for Pilgrim and Mayflower Management for office manager Bev Young. GMCR took the rest of the building.

The Pilgrim Partnership has proven to be a notable asset to Waterbury and surrounding communities. The building of Pilgrim Park created much for the economy, with a location for employment, incubation and growth for local businesses. The Pilgrims shared their wealth of resources and were fair to their tenants. They donated monetarily and volunteered throughout their lives, striving to make Waterbury one of the best places to live.

Many locals helped make the Pilgrims and Pilgrim Partnership successful. At the risk of leaving some out, the list of companies includes the Charlie O'Brien family, Joel Baker, Larry Westover, Kingsbury Construction, Grenier Engineering, G.W. Parker Electric, Joseph Greene Architects, McCain Consulting Services, Chris Viens, Charlie Forbes, Wayne Lamberton and others.

When it was time for the Pilgrims to retire, along came a few young men to continue their legacy by keeping their goals and dreams alive. Wayne Lamberton, Randy LaGue and Patrick Malone have become a new presence in Waterbury.

4

PERKINS-PARKER FUNERAL HOME AND CREMATION SERVICE

Christopher Palermo

Founded in 1907 by Vernon L. Perkins of Warren, V.L. Perkins Company Home Furnishers and Funeral Service operated as a furniture and dry goods store on the main floor at 46 South Main Street in Waterbury with the funeral home on the second floor. Following the marriage of Charles Parker to Norma Perkins, Vernon's daughter, Charles became a licensed mortician and succeeded Vernon following his passing. In the mid-1940s, Charles purchased the property next door, which functioned for many decades as the town's community hall. Originally the village firehouse, the building later became the town hall, hosting everything from high school basketball games to boxing matches, town meetings and plays on the second floor, with locker rooms on the first floor and two jail cells in the rear of the building. The building went dormant following the construction of a new gymnasium at the high school on Stowe Street and was renovated to become the funeral home in 1957.

Charles passed away in 1969, and his children, Craig "Rusty" Parker and Priscilla (Parker) Palermo, inherited the furniture store and funeral home. In 1979, great-grandson Chris Palermo was approached about becoming the next generation to work in the family business. A recent graduate of UVM, he agreed to come and work for a year to see if it was the right fit. On June 10, 1983, Chris purchased the furniture store and funeral home and, in 1991, closed the furniture store to focus solely on funeral service and developing the newly acquired monument business. Perkins-Parker Funeral

Home and Cremation Service continued to grow, providing service to an expanding number of families in the central Vermont area.

Life and business changed dramatically on the evening of August 28, 2011. Vermont, particularly along the spine of the Green Mountains, felt the torrential force of Tropical Storm Irene. Devastating floodwaters engulfed communities along the Mad and Winooski Rivers, including Waterbury Village. The funeral home, in a little over an hour, received three feet of water on the main floor and seven feet in the garages. Everything was lost: $100,000 worth of vehicles and everything inside the building. The saving grace was no one was in the care of the funeral home during the flood. Rebuilding everything from the basement to the ceiling of the first floor took four months of daily work. Throughout the reconstruction, the funeral home never missed a beat, continuing to provide services; it worked cooperatively with other funeral homes to do preparation, utilizing churches, parish halls and the American Legion to hold services. It was remarkable how the community came together with the help of volunteers from surrounding towns.

On September 21, 2020, following forty-one years in funeral service, thirty-seven of those years as a business owner, Chris decided it was time to retire and closed on the sale of the funeral home and all assets with Jim Kennedy, owner of Lavigne Funeral Home in Winooski.

The funeral home will continue to operate as Perkins-Parker Funeral Home and Cremation Service at its current location in Waterbury, and John Woodruff, my longtime and invaluable employee, will continue his vocation with Perkins-Parker. I am truly thankful for my years of service to the families of central Vermont and the trust and faith they put in me and those who worked with me. It's been a remarkable and fulfilling journey.

After 41 years and serving nearly four thousand families, I can unequivocally say that serving families in funeral service was the best decision I could have ever made. Four generations, 113 years of continued family ownership and management, it has been truly a remarkable journey and a vocation I have cherished every day. I am confident that moving forward, Perkins-Parker Funeral Home and Cremation Service will continue its strong tradition of helping families get where they need to be and those who have passed where they need to go.

5

WATERBURY SERVICE CENTER

Albert Caron

I have owned the Waterbury Service Center for the past twenty years, having purchased it in October 2000. The land and building were owned by Champlain Oil in Burlington, and the name was owned by Gary Reynolds in Middlesex. Prior to the purchase, I worked for Contractors Crane Service Inc. in Morrisville, and I was interested in owning my own business. One of my suppliers, Mark Sikora of Sikora Auto Parts in Richmond, told me Waterbury Service Center was for rent, and I was attracted to it because at that time it was a full-service Texaco station.

While in high school in Colebrook, New Hampshire, I worked in a Texaco station and realized what that station brought to my community. People did business there because of the slogan, "You can trust your car to the man under the star." That slogan is no longer used, but it stuck with me and, throughout my career as an auto mechanic, I always wanted to own a Texaco station. After getting the backing I needed, I purchased the land, building and name; here I am twenty years later, no longer selling gas but continuing the full service of repairing and maintaining all types of vehicles.

When I officially opened the business, I was a bit nervous, as I had no idea who my customer base was. Fortunately, it was approaching winter tire season and employees at the state complex supported my venture, which has continued to this day. That started my customer base, but once the tire season was done things slowed down.

It was then I met Isabelle Boyce, who was the director of the Waterbury Area Senior Center Association (WASCA), and Marge and Ron Gulyas, members of the Rotary Club of Waterbury and two of my earliest customers. These chance meetings helped both me and my business—because of them I began participating in the community.

I became involved with the food shelf, selling Christmas trees at the Wesleyan Church, working with students at Crossett Brook Middle School and assisting with fundraisers at Waterbury Area Senior Center, Rotary functions and the local garden club, A River Runs Through It (ARRTI). Also, I have helped raise money during the Big Change RoundUp for the UVM Children's Hospital. The Barre Vocational Technical Center contacted me to ask if I would help guide some of their students. One of those students had purchased a vehicle with a bad motor; I assisted and guided her with rebuilding it so it could run again. I hired two employees from Vermont's VocRehab program, which evolved into a valuable partnership and has helped us both.

When 9/11 happened, it was a difficult time for me. However, it provided an opportunity to think about what else I might do for my business community. Along with the Gulyas, I approached the Senior Center to inquire about hosting an appreciation dinner for the area seniors. The center agreed to have the dinner there, and Marge and Ron, having been in the food service business for many years, had the expertise to help make it happen. My goal was to hold a dinner for the seniors, showing them appreciation and thanking them for all they give to their families and communities. This was in memory of my grandmother. She gave me much during my childhood, and I made her a promise that one day, if I was in the right position, I would do something to thank other seniors.

Following that first dinner, I began to see more and more seniors come to my shop for service. Rene Kaegle was one of the first and named me Mr. Texaco. That made me proud, as did meeting many others, such as Mary Daudelin, who was so sweet and kind and treated me as her son. And the dinner? The annual Thanksgiving Dinner for Seniors continued for seventeen years. It was a celebration as much as a dinner. We provided, at no charge, a home-cooked, family-style dinner for seniors and members of their families, complete with carnation corsages, chocolates, music and gifts for every senior. For those who could not attend the dinner, we provided both takeout and delivery service. Almost everything was donated by community members and businesses. At this writing, we are experiencing the COVID-19 pandemic and, unfortunately, were not able to hold the dinner this year. We plan on hosting it next year.

The summer following that first dinner, I was invited to the Rotary changeover dinner, a celebration to thank the outgoing president and welcome the new one. However, the big surprise for me was that I was named their Businessperson of the Year, a true privilege and honor for me, as I consider Waterbury a special place to do business.

My business was hit hard during the economic downturn in 2008 and the subsequent Cash for Clunkers initiative. This program was intended to provide economic incentives to U.S. residents to purchase a new, more fuel-efficient vehicle by trading in a less efficient one. This removed older vehicles in need of repairs from the road and put new vehicles, needing fewer repairs and under warranty, on the road. Fewer repairs resulted in less business for me. I was ready to throw in the towel, and might have; however, my dad and Marge and Roy Gulyas convinced me that business would improve. Sure enough, in 2009 things started to turn around—until August 28, 2011, when Tropical Storm Irene arrived. My building was completely flooded, as were many other buildings in Waterbury. I had over $400,000 worth of damage. That was a huge setback, but the response from the community, my customers and my friends and family saved me once again. Volunteers arrived from other parts of the state and other parts of the country. People volunteered time and money, and many donated both.

After business was back on track, it was time for me to get involved in the community once again. This time it was with the Boy Scouts. In 2012, I started as assistant scoutmaster, continuing as scoutmaster of Troop 701 in Waterbury. I got involved in many of their outings and activities both at the local and district level. After volunteering to be on the camping committee for several years, I participated in Webelo's Woods, teaching basic outdoor survival skills. Webelo's stands for "WE'll BE LOyal Scouts" and is a two-year program for fourth and fifth graders. Together we camped at West Point in New York, where we watched the paratroopers, toured the campus and attended the Army-Navy football game. We went to Sturbridge Village in Massachusetts, where a living museum re-creates life in rural New England. Currently, I am the chair of the Eagle Board of Review, helping Scouts with their Eagle projects to attain the highest honor in scouting—Eagle Scout.

I have made numerous friends in the last twenty years, and some have even adopted me into their families. Waterbury isn't just any U.S. town. This is a community where people are who they say they are and stand up for one another. When I first came here, I didn't know what to expect, but I was told starting a business here would be the best choice I could make. The location, the population and just plain hometown pride and compassion have made this little town what it is today. As I look back at all Waterbury has given me, I wouldn't trade it for the world.

6

A WINDOW ONTO STOWE STREET

1990–2020

Jack Carter

For almost two hundred years, the area around Stowe and Main Streets has been the center of commerce for downtown Waterbury.

During the last quarter of the twentieth century, Stowe Street began to lose its vitality, beginning with the close of the ninety-year-old department store F.C. Luce Co. in 1985 and later the planned demolition of the now Stimson and Graves building to make room for a car wash. Stowe Street was also the once-busy Route 100. That distinction was lost when Route 100 was diverted to Exit 10 off Interstate 89, thus changing traffic flow away from the street to the interstate.

In the early 1990s, Revitalizing Waterbury and other investors saved the Stimson and Graves building from demolition and converted it into housing, retail and a senior center. This event led to the renaissance of new businesses on the block.

The Waterbury Senior Center was created by a group of senior citizens and other members of the community to offer a permanent home for that segment of the community and a place to meet, socialize and serve lunches on site along with the Meals on Wheels program. The first director was Isabelle Boyce, and the first head cook was Annie Coffey. Over the years, the center has seen many changes in staff and members but still serves as a vital part of the community. The center has also been a place for the public to hold events, also serving the community for that purpose.

Holiday window display at the Stowe Street Emporium gift shop located on Stowe Street in Waterbury. *Courtesy of Gordon Miller.*

In 1994, sisters Jan Chotalal and Wantee Bartlett opened Marsala Salsa Restaurant at 15 Stowe Street, serving Mexican and West Indian cuisine, a first for Waterbury. The restaurant closed in 2012, and the Blue Stone restaurant now occupies the space.

Also in 1994, Jack Carter and Ted Schultheis opened the Stowe Street Emporium at number 23 and did extensive renovations to the vacant storefront. In 2005, they expanded to number 21 with a store next door. They closed that store in 2010 and consolidated back to 23. In 2013, they sold the business to Kathy and Larry Murphy and their daughter, Kate Ruggles.

In 1995, Kyle Russell and Mike Carr opened KC's Bagel Café at 19 Stowe Street. This location was part of the former F.C. Luce Co. It is presently operated by Kyle and Buffy Garrand. All the while, the venerable radio station WDEV AM and FM, on the air since 1931, has set forth in the same location at number 9. WDEV is a treasure in our community and state.

Next door at 5 Stowe Street is Axel's Frame Shop & Gallery. Originally started by Axel Stohlberg across the street at number 10, it is now owned by Whitney Aldrich. The gallery is host to many local artists' exhibitions.

Another totally transformed building is One Stowe Street. In 2006, Christopher Tagatac restored the 1833 building. Originally called the Corner Store, it is the oldest commercial building in town. It is now home to offices on the top floors and the Blackback Pub on the lower floor with proprietors Lynn Mason and Dave Juenker.

At the other end of the block is 29 Stowe Street. Owner Sylvia Aylward rehabilitated the historic building. In 2009, Hiata Corduan Defeo opened Bridgeside Books in the front section of the building. Hiata created a mecca for book lovers, including a wonderful selection for children. All age groups enjoyed her welcoming personality. Book signings and readings are a feature of this shop. In 2020, the bookstore was sold to Katya d'Angelo and her husband, Chris Triolo.

Also in the building is Stowe Street Café, owned by Nicole Grenier and opened in 2015. Stephanie Biczko is the head chef. The café has been transformed from the 1950's Mid-State Alleys bowling venue to an attractive restaurant and art gallery. One can see the candlepin bowling alley lines on the floor.

In earlier days, Sylvia Aylward operated an exercise business called Locomotion Fitness Center and later Aylward Upholstery with Dana Marineau. The community takes delight in the building's flowers and landscaping, provided by Sylvia.

In 2001, the Waterbury Activities and Cultural Committee (WAAC) started the Stowe Street Arts Festival, which grew into the Waterbury Arts Fest. The arts festival had become a premier summer event, attracting thousands to the street for the two-day celebration. WAAC was founded in 1991 by a group of concerned residents, led by Janet DiBlasi, who wanted to encourage the arts and activities in the community. They held their meetings at the Senior Center. Some of the activities instituted by the group were screening classic movies, bridge instruction and organizing weekly games, the Harvest Moon Ball, music on the lake (the reservoir) and Art in the Park.

Beautification of the downtown is another positive development that has taken place in the last thirty years. Along the sidewalks, colorful flowers are planted in whiskey barrels in the summer and lighted garland in the winter. This project was started by some of the street's merchants and is now carried on by the Revitalizing Waterbury Design Committee.

The American Legion is at number 16 and is one of the longest occupants on Stowe Street. After a disastrous fire in 1986 that destroyed the building, originally the Waterbury Opera House, the Legion rebuilt on the site. Next to the Legion at number 28 is a new structure, built in 2020 as a mixed-use building.

At the northern edge of the block is the Dry Bridge, which was created as an overpass for the railroad. The current bridge was built in 2004 and 2005 to resemble the original 1914 bridge. The two-year project was a major enhancement to downtown.

Farther up the street, one project that had a lasting impact on the community was the renovation of the school into Brookside Primary School. The original building was erected as Waterbury High School in 1898. Over the years, it was the central school in town, and then in 1966 it became Waterbury Elementary School. In 2006 and 2007, it was transformed into TBPS at a cost of $7.8 million.

Another rehabilitation of a historic building was the Waterbury Feed Store, commonly called the Grist Mill, at 92 Stowe Street. The last remaining industrial building in the historic Mill Village District, the restored mill became the home of the Mist Grill restaurant and later Hen of the Wood restaurant. Custom Covers, an upholstery service, and Tabbatha Henry Designs have occupied spaces in the building.

No window onto Stowe Street would be complete without looking south from the Dry Bridge. Straight ahead is both One South Main Street and 2 North Main Street, both handsome classic Federal/Greek Revival nineteenth-century buildings. One South Main Street was built in 1834, as was its neighbor 2 North Main. Both have been occupied by many businesses over their lifetimes.

One South Main Street is the home to the restaurant The Reservoir, established in 2009 by Mark Frier. 2 North Main Street is owned by John and Val Vincent. For many years, it was Vincent's Drug Store, and it is now occupied by Sunflower Salon & Boutique, Kelly Richardson, proprietor.

Some of the other businesses on the street, over the past thirty years, not in business now or relocated, are:

1 South Main Street | Sisters Two, Thirsty Turtle, American Bistro, a coffee house, Waterbury Wings

2 North Main Street | Bisbee's Paint and Flooring, Five Hills Bike Shop

1 Stowe Street | Waterbury Pub, Great Wall Chinese Restaurant, Irie's Bike Shop, Stebu Sushi, Dick Messier's Barber Shop, Angelo's Deli, Ann's Weavery, Salon on Main (moved a few buildings down the street), Cork Wine Bar

5 Stowe Street | Couching Lion Book Store
9 Stowe Street | WCVT-FM (classical radio station)
10 Stowe Street | Waterbury Market (Steve Yandow), Martha Lewis Antiques
18 Stowe Street | Garland Insurance, JingJi's Dumpling Shop
19 Stowe Street | Harold's Cheesecake Shop, Shear Perfection, Sunflower Salon (moved to 2 North Main)
21 Stowe Street | Video Exchange, Vermont Handcrafters, Angelo's Deli, Vermont Tibetan Rugs, Ruelle Boutique (moved to 23 Stowe Street)
23 Stowe Street | Coffin's TV
29 Stowe Street | Katie's Jewels, Tabbatha Henry Ceramics, C. Michael Dudash Artist Studio, Jazzercise

Some of the current businesses on the street other than those previously listed are:

1 Stowe Street | Ursa Major, Third Planet Wind Power
5 Stowe Street | American Canadian Tour (upstairs)
10 Stowe Street | Tabbatha Henry Designs
21 Stowe Street | Lasting Image Salon, Donna Boring's Sewing Room, LaStrada Bakery
23 Stowe Street | Winooski Masonic Lodge (upstairs)

With completion of the reconstruction of Main Street and the first block of Stowe Street in 2021, no doubt the window onto Stowe Street will look even better in the next thirty years. It certainly has changed for the better in the last thirty years.

PART IV

CELEBRATIONS AND EVENTS

1
RIVER OF LIGHT LANTERN PARADE

MK Monley

The River of Light Lantern Parade in Waterbury, Vermont, was conceived in 2010. Artist Gowri Savoor, along with the engineering mind of artist Angelo Arnold, introduced the concept as a collaboration with Thatcher Brook Primary School (now Brookside Elementary School) art teacher MK Monley. Celebrating the spirit of community-engaged art, this tradition has expanded creatively and attracted participants and viewers from surrounding communities each year.

Our first River of Light parade in 2010 was held on a weekday evening in mid-December as a school-wide event. There were big, fat, beautiful, fluffy snowflakes softly landing everywhere. The magic of the event and the delight of all participants were obvious, and a tradition was born. This first year, the children paraded and the parents were the spectators. The parade route that year followed Stowe Street to Railroad Street to Rusty Parker Park, where a school-wide musical performance was held. We then reversed course up Railroad Street and back to the school.

The next year, Tropical Storm Irene hit, August 28, 2011. Our town was devastated, with significant destruction. I remember sitting in my classroom the week following the flood, realizing the state of the streets and our town would not support a parade in December. On cue, Gowri Savoor assured me that we could hold the parade and that more than ever, this was what our community needed. She was right. The theme for that year was *Flight*. Students made large origami cranes whose bodies carried lights, and along with other flight-themed lanterns, a group of us built a giant phoenix. Her name was Ophelia, and she became the symbol of rebuilding our town after the flood.

After that first year, families and groups of friends and coworkers joined their children creating lanterns and walking in the parade. It was no longer just a "kids do it and parents watch" event; it had evolved into an event in which all ages contribute and collaborate. In 2012 our theme was *Outer Space*. There's a beautiful article about the parade from Eve Sollberger in *Seven Days*. If you watch this video, you'll see the amazingly gleeful atmosphere that the parade brings to our community. Summing up the quotes from this video, people feel that the parade has become a tradition. It is full of joy, is accessible to everyone no matter their age, is magical, is a testament to the value of art in the schools and community and is a community-building event. The quote that sums it up for me is from a first grader in 2011: "It just makes my heart feel glad on this lantern parade."

From 2013 to 2019, the River of Light established a parade route that started at Thatcher Brook Primary School and ended at Dac Rowe Park. With the help of the town recreation department and a host of community volunteers, a bonfire, warming fires, hot chocolate and fire spinners welcomed the throngs of parade participants.

A global pandemic arrived in March 2020. Schools closed, and children did not return until after Labor Day 2020; they came back on a very limited basis, with strict health and safety guidelines. No gatherings were permitted. It was clear that the River of Light Lantern Parade would not proceed as usual. It was clear that 2020, our parade's eleventh year, would be the time to try something different. We enlisted the art teachers from the surrounding schools and started planning.

An idea evolved: All participants would make their lanterns and erect them in three different locations. Instead of a moving parade through Waterbury, attendees would drive (and walk on a designated, socially distanced, safe path) through the lantern parade. The sites were staged in Dac Rowe Park in Waterbury Village, the driveway of Crossett Brook Middle School and at Camp Meade next to Red Hen Bakery in Middlesex.

This socially distanced approach to keeping this much-loved parade tradition was a success. The theme for 2020 was *Brave Little State*, reflecting the many things about which to be brave during this time. Joining together as a community to collectively share our individual light brought much joy in this darkest of times.

Participants in the Annual River of Light parade march down Stowe and Main Streets in downtown Waterbury. *Courtesy of Gordon Miller.*

River of Light Themes

2010: *First Light*
2011: *Flight*
2012: *Outer Space*
2013: *Sea Creatures*
2014: *Our Town*
2015: *Bugs*
2016: *Plants*
2017: *Sound*
2018: *Food*
2019: *ReInventions*
2020: *Brave Little State*

Many musicians have contributed their talents to our parades throughout the years, with the most consistent and memorable support coming from a Burlington-based irresistibly rhythmic street band, Sambatucada, and the Crossett Brook Middle School Junk Band. They move within the parade and continue to delight the crowd in Dac Rowe Park at the end of the parade, alongside the bonfires, fire spinners Ignus Solus and Cirque de Fuego and party atmosphere.

Throughout the years, the parade organizers have been invaluable to the success of the parade. They are Gowri Savoor, lead artist; Angelo Arnold, lead artist; MK Monley, lead teacher; Mame McKee, teaching artist; Sarah-Lee Terrat, teaching artist; and Nick Nadeau, recreation director.

2

WATERBURY ARTS FEST

Karen Nevin

Revitalizing Waterbury (RW), a nonprofit organization dedicated to creating and maintaining a vibrant community, hosts an annual two-day festival. The Waterbury Arts Fest (Saturday) is an outdoor event with nearly one hundred art exhibitors, live music and a variety of eatery options. The Friday Night Block Party is a large dance party held the evening before with live entertainment, a beer garden, food trucks and dancing. The entire event takes place on Stowe Street and Bidwell Lane in Waterbury the second weekend in July. The streets are closed for the event.

The Waterbury Arts Fest (WAF) serves as RW's only fundraiser of the year, raising funds that support economic development activities, regional marketing and promotion, community programming and outreach and direct support of local businesses. Waterbury is also a Vermont Designated Downtown and provides municipal support for community-wide projects.

Friday Night Block Party

The Friday Night Block Party is RW's way of saying thank you to the community for their support. It is a free event (donations accepted) held in the center of historic downtown. A main stage is set up, a beer garden is hosted by a local restaurant and food trucks such as Skinny Pancake and

Cornerstone Pub offer fabulous fare to eat. Each year a band is chosen that will get everyone up and dancing under the stars. Approximately 2,500 people attend the Friday Night Block Party.

Waterbury Arts Fest

On Saturday, artists and craftsmen line the closed Stowe Street and Bidwell Lane. Artists are chosen for quality and range of art mediums. Each year, the artists' work includes fine art painting, pottery, fiber art, weaving, glasswork, baskets, jewelry, woodwork and sculpture. Many artists conduct demonstrations throughout the day. Interspersed with the artists are a variety of fun food vendors that tempt all palates. The main stage has performances throughout the day, including local favorites, the dancers from Green Mountain Performing Arts. Saturday's events are free for all ages.

This is a community-centric event that celebrates the arts, music and Waterbury. Revitalizing Waterbury's mission is to preserve, promote and enhance the economic, historic and social vitality of our town.

3

WATERBURY WINTERFEST

Roger Clapp

Waterbury Winterfest is a community celebration of Vermont's longest season. The midwinter annual event has expanded from a handful of outdoor activities in 2011 to thirty-five events attracting two thousand participants over a ten-day stretch in 2020, starting the last weekend in January and concluding the first weekend in February. A nine-member volunteer leadership team solicits support from area merchants and coordinates activities, both outdoors and indoors, with event leaders to share the Waterbury winter experience with the local community and beyond. With low overhead, Waterbury Winterfest has been able to use event proceeds to support Waterbury recreation, giving out over twenty-five grants to local organizations. While the current COVID-19 pandemic presents new challenges to plans for the ten-year anniversary event, this brief history provides some context for this Waterbury community initiative.

Waterbury Winterfest (WF) was initiated by the Town of Waterbury's Recreation Committee in 2011 in collaboration with a regional Nordic ski competition staged on the Dac Rowe fields. Peg O'Neill was one of the key organizers that first year, and in succeeding years the Peg O'Neill Trophy has been awarded to the most active participant at the conclusion of Winterfest events.

In the wake of the 2011 flood, the Waterbury Recreation Committee encouraged the community to "Rebound with Recreation" in January 2012. Opening ceremonies were moved up to MLK weekend to correspond with

Waterbury's traditional family skate on the outdoor rink and Xmas tree bonfire at Anderson Park. Bill Minter took on a leading role, and WF events were expanded to include broomball, a fun run and a Snow Ball dance party with media coverage provided by WDEV and the *Waterbury Record*. An ad hoc WF organizational committee was formed to continue building WF events with support from the town, participants and local merchant sponsors who suggested the event could fill the lull between the MLK and Presidents Week holidays. Organizers came to recognize the value of having two weekends to cover the vagaries of winter weather. So WF has evolved into a ten-day midwinter celebration to improve access to recreational opportunities for the Waterbury community and beyond.

Expansion of activities has increased both indoors and out. Outdoor events have included a seven-mile backcountry descent on skis and snowshoes from Blush Hill to Little River, snow football and more recently snow volleyball. Indoor events include the ever-popular Game Show organized by Chad Ummel and Natalie Sherman, a beer tasting competition at the Blackback Pub, storytelling and musical events at the Grange Hall in Waterbury Center.

In 2012, Waterbury hired a new recreation director, Chad Ummel, who added a burst of energy and creativity into the program. He designed a WF website and helped increase community involvement through increased visibility and awareness. In 2016, the town Recreation Committee recognized the need for WF, the new dog park and other organizations to manage finances outside of the town budget. They helped to create Friends for Waterbury Area Recreation Development (FORWARD) as a 501(c)3 sponsoring organization.

The relationship with FORWARD has allowed WF to continue as a volunteer organization and raise sponsorship support from local businesses with tax-exempt status. WF has been able to retain and direct funding from year to year and formalize a grant making program. Since the beginning, WF has been providing scholarship support for needy families to participate in the Waterbury Rec Summer Program. The expanded grants program provided grants of $500 to $2,000 to Waterbury-area recreation programs providing opportunities for kids and others to enjoy soccer, dancing, hockey, mountain biking, baseball and adaptive sports. Beneficiaries have been encouraged to participate in WF, helping to introduce new offerings, including snow soccer, Big Toy night and a biathlon.

Waterbury Winterfest was preparing to celebrate its tenth anniversary in January 2021 with a mission to enhance public recreation opportunities by providing venues for people to come and enjoy winter with others from the Waterbury community and beyond. WF leadership currently includes nine volunteer members and four elected officers to manage WF business. Independent event leaders are recruited each fall to plan and develop programs, attract participants and generate revenue for WF with guidance from the WF leadership team. The global COVID-19 pandemic has caused organizers to temporarily suspend normal activities, but a committed group of WF volunteers expects Winterfest will continue once social gathering restrictions are relaxed.

The Wanderlust Challenge: Winterfest's Response to the COVID Pandemic of 2020–21

After a growing number of participants had come to discover the magic of a Waterbury winter, the COVID pandemic of 2020–21 threatened to shut the whole thing down. Winterfest organizers had to screw on their thinking caps to come up with a plan that complied with the new safety protocols. So, leadership team member Eric Weeber worked with Vermont park ranger Chad Ummel to develop the Wanderlust Challenge with over

A sample of the varied winter activities held at Anderson Field's skating rink, located off Butler Street in Waterbury. The Waterbury Winterfest Committee plans activities annually. *Courtesy of Gordon Miller.*

seventy-five options for individuals and families to explore, create, give back or just hunker down.

Eager for a new creative outlet during the pandemic, the community responded to this new scavenger hunt challenge, posting over 1,190 photos of wild turkeys crossing the yard, their dog at the dog park, kids catching snowflakes on their tongues, knitting a pair of mittens, summiting nearby mountains and shoveling their neighbor's walk. From the end of January through the month of February, fifty teams competed for weekly prizes provided by sixteen local sponsoring businesses. Special prizes were awarded for best homemade game, best dance video, best snow fort and best ice cream made from snow.

Winterfest worked with local sponsors, adding prizes for images of canned goods from local breweries, bank signs and the iconic vehicles of SunCommon. Winterfest bought a fat bike to encourage people to explore Waterbury trails at reduced rates and staged a "Name that Fat Bike" contest. This all-weather two-wheeler will now be known as "Winterfest Wander Wheels," or WWW for short. The Winterfest leadership team would like to thank all participants and sponsors supporting the event throughout our ten-year history. We will be further supporting Waterbury recreation through our grants program in spring 2021 and count on rebounding with in-person events for Winterfest 2022 and beyond.

4

WATERBURY HISTORICAL SOCIETY'S MEMORIAL DAY GHOST WALK

Jan Gendreau

It was the early 2000s, when my husband, Don, and I went to Peacham's July Fourth celebration. *Vermont Life* had advertised that they were having a ghost walk—I was intrigued, and I wasn't disappointed! I returned to Waterbury thinking our historical society needed to do something similar. Celebrating Waterbury Historical Society's fiftieth anniversary in 2007 was the perfect opportunity. What started as a special event has become a tradition.

Each year, we gather at 11:00 a.m. on Memorial Day. We join the American Legion in a traditional service, placing a wreath in honor of veterans. An original composition or favorite piece of prose or poetry is presented by a middle school student. Sometimes we sing a song.

Following this, we divide into three or four groups and visit the graves of our featured honorees and hear how they have made an impact on our community. Each year, a different cemetery is visited: Hope, the Old Cemetery on Route 100, Maple Street, Loomis Hill and Holy Cross in Duxbury. There are additional cemeteries in Waterbury, but they are on private land or are not accessible to the general public.

Typically, a walk has a theme: the early settlers (families of Gregg, Guptil, Wallace, Jones in the Old Route 100 Cemetery); another year featured Marsh, Butler, Dillingham and Austin families in Hope.

Did you ever wonder where Harwood Union High School got its name, or who was F.C. Luce, who had the store on Stowe Street? Who was Harry

Jack Carter, member of the Historical Society, shares stories of the ghost of Ezra Butler during the annual Ghost Walk in Waterbury's Hope Cemetery. *Courtesy of Skip Flanders.*

Cutting, and why did the American Legion name Post 59 after him? And what was the story behind Perkins-Parker funeral home? Or why is there an historical marker in front of the library?

The year 2011 marked the 150th anniversary of the beginning of the Civil War. Linda Radtke, singer/researcher, dressed in period costume and shared Vermont songs from the Civil War period. We found forty-two veterans of that war in Hope Cemetery alone. The next year, we learned of the thirty-seven Civil War veterans in the Rte. 100 Cemetery, the Godfrey and Sleeper families sending three and four sons to fight and return.

We celebrated the restoration of the Loomis Hill Cemetery in 2014. Barb Walton, her Latter-day Saints volunteers, some of her grandchildren and several historical society members took on the repair and placement of monuments, cleared the weeds, thinned the trees and reclaimed the beautiful little cemetery. A marker was placed at the entrance with the names of people buried there in the nineteenth century. So, we spent time getting to know Silas Loomis and other folks who settled Waterbury Center.

In Holy Cross, we found folks who had come to Waterbury after emigrating from Ireland and Lebanon; the Harveys and Izors were successful entrepreneurs and community politicians. The first resident priest in Waterbury, Father Galigan, is here. John Lafayette, MIA; Buddy Truax, traveling musician; and Nap DeGuise, barber/inventor/artist were featured during another visit.

Special ladies in Maple Street Cemetery were Gladys Wrisley, Lizzie Minot, Anne Witham, Winona Hoffman and Helen Burleigh. Veterans were also remembered in the same cemetery: Herbert Hunt Jr., George Woodard and Rex Morse.

In 2018, we featured the 1918 flu pandemic and learned how it affected the Wallace family and Dr. Wasson, who was infected and died because he took care of patients at the Vermont State Hospital. We never imagined we would experience a worldwide pandemic in 2020.

Sometimes we find descendants of the people we are featuring. If we are fortunate enough to have them tell us about their ancestors, they often come to us after and thank us for the opportunity to learn and celebrate. History is so much more than dates and politics. Our walks through the cemeteries give us a chance to put faces to events and become acquainted with local history one person at a time.

5

WINTER CROQUET (WDEV)

Charlotte Strasser

After thirty-five years, Winter Croquet came to an end in 2019. Begun on March 9, 1985, by morning host Mike Carey and station manager Tom Beardsley, the game was played every March at Rusty Parker Memorial Park in snow, rain or mud. The game's original guidelines prohibited cheating, but in years to follow, cheating would not only be accepted but also encouraged.

Poet Laureate of "Music to Go to the Dump By," Lew D'Array, penned a poem for the event. In 2001, he wrote:

There once was a man on the go
Who hosted a radio show.
This son of a gun
Thought would be great fun
To play croquet in the snow.

The thing about being in Vermont
Is that people just do what they want.
It's O.K. they're confused
As long as they're amused
So out to the park they did jaunt.

Seven teams showed up; yup they came
To seek their fortune and fame.
Not being completely the fools
They ignored or challenged the rules
And simply invented their own game.

The snow was crusted with ice
And some fell through more than twice.
Their opponents just jeered
The spectators cheered
While their teammates offered advice.

One by one the teams did fall out
Accompanied by laughs and a shout.
At last there was only one team
Who achieved the elusive dream.
The Rotary had won
'Twas all in good fun
And that's what this game is about.

Each year, a celebrated official of officials presided over the game, including then lieutenant governor Phil Scott in 2014. The winning team became trustee of the rotating trophy for a year. Rotating it was—literally. The trophy was created by the artists at Jack's Body Shop in Morrisville using an old car rim, two croquet mallets, balls and a music box. Originally, the trophy rotated while playing Christmas carols backward, but either due to time or overuse the trophy eventually ceased rotating. It continued, however, to make the rounds of the various winners.

1985	Howard Bank
1986	The Bungle Family
1987	VT Realty Exchange "Sticky Wickets"
1988	Glasswork's Wormburners
1989	The Bungle Family
1990	The Bungle Family
1991	Waterbury Fire Department
1992	Known Knights- Knights of Columbus
1993	Waterbury Fire Department Auxiliary
1994	Sullivan Powers "1040 E-Z's"

1995 Glasswork's Wormburners
1996 Waterbury Fire Department
1997 Waterbury Fire Department
1998 Sons of the American Legion
1999 Waterbury Fire Department
2000 Waccy Wickets
2001 Waterbury Rotary Club
2002 Waterbury Fire Department
2003 Waterbury Fire Department
2004 Waterbury Fire Department
2005 Waterbury Fire Department
2006 Waterbury Rotary
2007 Waterbury Fire Department
2008 Wicket Wesleys
2009 Waterbury Fire Department
2010 Lamoille Union High School Croquet Society
2011 The Club (Navy Midshipmen from U.S. Naval Academy–Annapolis)
2012 Waterbury Rotary Belly Academy Team 2
2013 Out for Blood Zombies Among Us
2014 The Udder Guys
2015 The Udder Guys
2016 Waterbury Fire Department
2017 Waterbury Fire Department
2018 The Alchemist
2019 The E-Fudders

PART V

COMMUNICATIONS AND MEDIA

1

EXIT 10, 1988–2008

Anne M. Imhoff

In January 1988, Steve VanEsen called a meeting of Waterbury residents to form an "all-volunteer publication of, by, and for the people of Waterbury."

The first twelve-page, 8½" x 11" issue of the *Waterbury News* went in the mail for February/March 1988. Chris Smith, the first editor, oversaw twenty-five individuals who worked on and contributed to the issue. The newsletter featured articles about what was happening in Waterbury in addition to business notes, special events, Waterbury churches and a community calendar.

Most importantly, the issue carried an insert, Name the Newsletter Contest. With ninety-three entries, judging was difficult. Mariana Towne's *Exit 10* was judged best, as it described the community the newsletter reached—Duxbury and Waterbury. For the first seven years, *Exit 10* was published bimonthly by community volunteers who rotated as editors, writers, advertising salespeople and bill collectors, with the senior citizens stuffing the newsletter into envelopes at the Waterbury Center Fire Station.

In March 1994, at a community meeting moderated by Reverend Paul Willard, it was voted Anne M. Imhoff would be the publisher and editor of *Exit 10*. Imhoff changed *Exit 10* from a bimonthly newsletter to a monthly newspaper but continued it as an all-volunteer endeavor, with the assistance of community members writing articles, collecting ads and copy and submitting the work to Imhoff for final editing and printing preparation.

Banner advertising Waterbury's local newspaper *Exit 10*, started by publisher and editor Anne M. Imhoff in 1988. The paper folded in 2008. *Courtesy of Anne M. Imhoff.*

Many changes in the community took place through the years. In 2000, featured articles were the sale of Cold Hollow Cider Mill by Francine and Eric Chittenden to Paul and Gayle Brown, WDEV's Y2K Winter Croquet winners, the thirty-first annual *Ground Hog Opry* with Radio Hot Shots Roland Uphill and Neil Downs from WSMM (Well Shut My Mouth) Radio, the opening of the Women's Residential Treatment Facility at the State Hospital, dedication of the Korean and Vietnam War monuments in Rusty Parker Memorial Park, the deterioration of the Waterbury dam and draft plans for its repair. Issues carried the obituaries of Reverend Louis R. Logue, twenty-five-year veteran and fire chief Edward J. Eldredge and Raymond "Doc" Dumas.

Waterbury dam repairs, the 200th anniversary of the Waterbury Congregational Church, building the Ice Center, Waterbury Medical Center's move to a new building on South Main Street and the repair and conversion into sixteen units of affordable housing in the old Green Mountain Seminary purchased from the Eric and Francine Chittenden by Central Vermont Community Land Trust were some of the news in 2003. Additionally, that year included the start of Waterbury Backcountry Rescue Team, the 75th anniversary of the 1927 flood, dedication of the new fire department tower truck as the Donald I. LaRock Tower Company, retirement of Francis "Bubby" Wilder after 32 years of service as a Waterbury employee and a celebration of the life of Dr. Henry Janes.

Major fires destroyed the 152-year-old Wells house, known as the Gateway Motel (2002), and the Green Mountain Club's barn. A house fire in June 2003 led to the death of twelve-year-old Jessica Peck, followed by the Coffin Building (2005) and Sir Richard's Antiques (2006).

Village fire captain Sally Dillon was named the Central Vermont Home Town Hero in April 2004. In June, The Children's Room celebrated twenty years of operation. Revitalizing Waterbury signed a thirty-year lease to restore the train station. Major General Harold Denny Campbell's monument was dedicated at Rusty Parker Memorial Park, and Scott Wells, Tom Cahalan and Nate Lord were welcomed home after serving tours in Afghanistan and Iraq. The end of 2004 saw the closure of the Ideal Market by Maxi and Marge Irish after thirty-eight years of operation seven days a week and the repairs and restoration of the 1859 St. Andrew Catholic Church.

The Stowe Street dry bridge was reconstructed in 2005, and Railroad Street was paved its entire length (2005–06). The Duxbury Food Shelf opened, and Duxbury built a new town garage. The Waterbury Library Commissioners closed the Waterbury Center library in December, and Anne Moeykens's (1928–2005) obituary appeared. The appearance of Main Street in Waterbury improved as new businesses took over several of the older village houses.

The year 2005 was a banner one for construction in town. Seven new, or added on to, buildings added a total of 105,483 square feet of new space to the Waterbury Grand List. Restorations or conversions of other buildings added an additional 20,320 square feet. Taken together, a rough overall estimate of $20 million in new construction went on the grand list.

Four merger votes for Waterbury town and village occurred over the years, and Waterbury received Designated Downtown status in 2006. WDEV (Waterbury Delights Every Visitor) celebrated its seventy-fifth anniversary, and the beautifully restored Waterbury railroad station opened in October 2006.

During 2007, discussions began for new fire stations; Gary Dillion, Ken Sargent, LeeAnne Viens and Celia Clark were profiled in the paper. Ed Steele and Ken Squier were honored by the community, and Dr. Jane Goodall visited Green Mountain Coffee Roasters. After the P&C market closed, RJ's Market opened in its place and Thatcher Brook Primary School was retrofitted, including a new entrance. The obituary of Patricia "Trish" K. Feld, school librarian, was published.

Ken Sabin passed away in January 2008 and Charles J. Adams in May. During the following months, Chief Wolfe left the village police department and was replaced by Joby Feccia. Wally Roberts stepped down as director of the Senior Center and Robert Dostis as our state representative. Waterbury Center Community Church celebrated its 175th anniversary while building began on a new Green Mountain Club barn, along Route 100. Coffin's TV and Rentals closed its doors in September.

In addition to physical changes, new organizations formed, offering events for our enjoyment, vital to our communities' quality of life. The Farmers Market provides fresh produce and a gathering place in the summer followed by Thursday evening concerts sponsored by the Rotary. The Waterbury Activities and Cultural Center sponsored films, lectures, dances, concerts and the annual Stowe Street Arts Festival until Revitalizing Waterbury took over management of the festival.

The Rotary Club has sponsored Easter egg hunts and parades, the Home & Garden Shows, the Hunt for Sunzilla and Santa in the Park. Other events included volunteers hitting the roads and byways each Green Up Day, A-River-Runs-Through-It Garden Club beautifying our towns in the summer and the Clyde Whittemore Little League and KidsFest celebrating our younger folks. These and older established events were reported regularly because *Exit 10* remained an "all-volunteer publication of, by and for the people of Waterbury and Duxbury."

With the business communities advertising support, *Exit 10* was able to appear monthly in everyone's mailbox. The minutes from the various boards that served our two communities, candidate forums, election results, special events, new business openings and other news articles were in each issue.

Exit 10 folded its pages with the December 2008 issue. Then the *Stowe Reporter* revived the *Waterbury Record* for several years until it too folded. Now we are in the digital age, and the *Waterbury Roundabout*, under the guidance of Lisa Scagliotti, is providing weekly news via the web. She too is relying on community members and students to keep us abreast of life in our towns. It is amazing what our towns, our volunteers and our businesses have accomplished in twenty years.

2

FRONT PORCH FORUM

Michael Wood-Lewis

Front Porch Forum (FPF) is a Vermont public benefit corporation that hosts online local forums in every community in the state. Started by couple Valerie and Michael Wood-Lewis in their Five Sisters Burlington neighborhood in 2000, they formed a business in 2006 and expanded to fifty neighborhoods in greater Burlington.

On the heels of Tropical Storm Irene, FPF expanded to Waterbury, launching on November 1, 2011. By February 2021, 4,269 local people had become members of the Waterbury FPF (out of the approximately 2,210 households there). Over this near decade of use, local people wrote 54,209 postings that were published across 3,686 daily issues.

In addition to thousands of neighbors, hundreds of local businesses, nonprofits, government agencies and elected officials participate. They post a wide variety of topics, including lost pets, plumber recommendations, block parties, public meeting announcements, school budget debates, bikes for sale, free strollers and so much more. Years of daily neighborly exchange had solved immediate problems and built social capital among neighbors.

3

WATERBURY RECORD PUBLISHES ITS LAST ISSUE

The Waterbury Record

Published March 26, 2020

After 13 years of publication (started in 2007), this will be the last issue of the Waterbury Record.
The Vermont Community Newspaper Group, based in Stowe, Morrisville, and South Burlington is suspending publication of the weekly community newspaper.

"Clearly, this decision is precipitated by the coronavirus crisis, but it's also about economics," said publisher Greg Popa. "The Record has never been profitable, but we were in this for the long haul. We started publishing the paper in 2007 to fill a news desert in a community we felt was on the upswing."

"Sadly, that never translated into widespread advertising support essential to any newspaper's survival, and the coronavirus pandemic has accelerated what we hoped would never happen, the suspension of operations in any of the communities we serve."

The *Waterbury Record* was not new to central Vermont journalism. A weekly by that name was started in 1895, with Harry C. Whitehill as editor and manager. Whitehill later became the owner of the paper and started WDEV radio.

In later years, U.S. Senator Patrick Leahy's parents published the newspaper until they founded Leahy Press in Montpelier in 1946.

The diminutive notice of the newspaper's own demise a year later jockeyed for front-page space with weekly chronicling of town doings, newly married and newly departed on October 16, 1947.

"Lack of help has been a major problem ever since The Record was taken over by the present management six years ago this week," wrote Milton Sunderland, the editor. "It was our hope that the end of the war would end that difficulty, but such was not the case."

This week, Popa wondered aloud: "Did we fail? Only the community can answer that question, but this suspension of operations is certainly no reflection on the many exceptional journalists who've worked at the Record over the past dozen years, covering countless school and municipal meetings, breaking news, school sports and people."

Some of those journalists included photojournalist Gordon Miller, reporters Monica Mead, Kristen Fountain, Chris Preston, Nathan Burgess, Josh O'Gorman, Andrew Martin, Maddie Hughes, Mike Verillo and Maria Archangelo, who became the retooled paper's first editor and publisher in 2007.

Archangelo went on to become publisher of the company, which at the time also included the *Stowe Reporter* and two magazines.

It had long been a dream for Biddle Duke, former owner and publisher of the *Stowe Reporter*, to bring the *Waterbury Record* back to Waterbury.

"Launching a paper is a wonderful thing for a community," Duke said in 2007. "The paper will be a dynamic work in progress, and that's part of the thrill. If it's working right, every week the pages will reflect the conversations, letters, thoughts, ideas and, yes, even complaints of the people who've taken the time to contribute to their paper. Because, in the end, weekly papers belong to their communities."

While initial plans called for opening a small office in Waterbury, the economics just never materialized, Popa said. Until the week it closed, the Vermont Community Newspaper Group published six weeklies with a total circulation of forty-two thousand.

The *Waterbury Record*, with a circulation of 4,500, published every Thursday, and was mailed to every home and business in Waterbury, Waterbury Center and parts of Duxbury. It had an initial circulation of four thousand.

"Needless to say, the entire crew is really disappointed right now," Popa said.

4

WATERBURY ROUNDABOUT

Lisa Scagliotti

Waterbury Roundabout is a volunteer effort created to provide local news coverage after the local weekly paper, the *Waterbury Record*, folded in late March 2020.

Overseeing and contributing to coverage are Waterbury residents Lisa Scagliotti and Gordon Miller. A longtime news reporter and editor in Vermont, Scagliotti mentors student journalists at the University of Vermont (UVM). A familiar face at many local events, Miller is a professional news and commercial photographer whose work was a staple in the *Record*. Each devotes time to a number of community organizations.

Contributing to this project are UVM student journalists from the Community News Service project, part of UVM's Reporting and Documentary Storytelling program in the Center for Research on Vermont. UVM senior Julia Bailey-Wells designed and maintains the site.

In 2020, over 1,300 community folk received copies via email. Subsequently, the *Waterbury Roundabout* collaborated with the *Times Argus*, a central Vermont newspaper, to publish a weekly paper called the *Waterbury Reader*.

5

WDEV RADIO VERMONT

Charlotte Strasser

WDEV, the brainchild of Harry Whitehill, signed on the airwaves on July 16, 1931. After the death of Whitehill in 1935, the station passed to William Ricker and Lloyd Squier in 1937. Ownership passed to Lloyd's son, Kenley Squier, in 1979. What began as a one-hour broadcast on a fifty-watt AM station located at frequency 1420 has grown to a five-thousand-watt AM station now at 550 on the dial along with a twenty-thousand-watt FM simulcast at 96.1, 96.5 and 98.3.

The year 2000 ended with changes at WDEV. Longtime WDEV employee Mike Carey retired, citing health reasons. Carey started at WDEV as a teen answering phones for *The Green Mountain Ballroom*. In 1984, Carey was promoted to sign on the station and host *Once Around the Clock* from 5:00 a.m. to 6:00 a.m. and *The Morning News Servic*e from 7:00 a.m. to 8:00 a.m., eventually adding the *Trading Post* program. In April 1994, Carey was teamed with radio group Vice President and General Manager Eric Michaels for a 6:00 a.m. to 9:00 a.m. morning news program known as *Wake Up, Vermont with Michael and Michaels.*

Following Carey's retirement, Dana Jewell hosted mornings. He introduced a yearly remote broadcast the opening day of deer rifle season from the ABCD Deer Camp in uptown Duxbury. Over the years, the deer camp welcomed guests including Governor Jim Douglas, Representative Danny Gore, George Woodard and Governor Phil Scott to enjoy some of the camp cook's hash and trade some laughs.

On a scorching hot July 16, 2006, WDEV celebrated seventy-five years with an ice cream social at Rusty Parker Park. Entertainment was provided by the Radio Rangers and Barre's Native Tongue. Dignitaries in attendance included Senator Patrick Leahy, Governor Jim Douglas and Representative Bernie Sanders. The event was organized by Jon Noyes, who would take over the morning reins from Dana Jewell two years later and remain in that position for ten years.

The guiding principle of WDEV since the beginning—Vermonters serving Vermonters—was put into practice on the evening of August 28, 2011. The deluge from Tropical Storm Irene caused rivers across Vermont to jump their banks, flooding communities and leaving some Vermonters cut off. Early in the evening, as floodwaters began rising in Waterbury village, the station at 9 Stowe Street lost power and the internet. The generator kicked in to keep the station on the air, but with no access to email, station manager Eric Michaels urged listeners to call his personal cellphone. Throughout the evening, listeners would text or call with updates, pleas for help or just to connect with others who were also victims of Mother Nature. Sign-off time usually came at midnight, but the team of Eric Michaels, Tom Beardsley, Lee Kittell and weather forecaster Roger Hill stayed on. The generator worked into the night, but during the early hours of the morning it was running out of fuel. Michaels alerted listeners that the station would have to shut down for a few minutes to refuel. Staff refueled the generator, and then the broadcast continued. When the team finally rested, they had been on the air for twenty-eight continuous hours.

For decades, the 9:00 a.m. to 11:00 a.m. weekday time slot has been dedicated to a locally produced public affairs call-in program. From 1999 to 2015, *The Mark Johnson Show* filled those hours. When Johnson left to pursue an editorial position at VTDigger.com, former Douglas secretary of administration and secretary of human services Mike Smith filled the position with *Open Mic*. Dave Gram, a former AP journalist, took over the program in 2018.

The year 2011 saw a shuffling of staff with the retirement of veteran broadcaster Jack Donovan. Donovan had started at WDEV in 1972. His *Vermont Live* series of broadcasts during the 1970s spotlighted local musicians. In 1987, Donovan's work was honored for his contribution to Vermont musicians and artists. He was promoted to program director in 1996 and began cohosting *Music to Go to the Dump By* in 1991. Donovan was inducted into the Vermont Association of Broadcasters Hall of Fame in 2010. Lee

Kittell moved from nights to afternoons to fill Donovan's spot. Donovan would continue to work Saturday mornings in his retirement.

Kittell began his career at WDEV in 1999 working from 4:00 p.m. to midnight and hosting *Score*, a sports talk and rock show. In 2018, Kittell moved to mornings, hosting *Once Around the Clock* and the morning and midday news services.

Station management underwent a change in 2017, when sales manager Steve Cormier replaced Eric Michaels. Michaels had been at WDEV since 1987. During his tenure, the Radio Vermont Group holdings were expanded to include WDEV-FM in Warren, WCVT-FM in Stowe, WLVB-FM in Morrisville and WEXP-FM in Rutland, along with FM translators in Barre and Island Pond. He was inducted into the Vermont Association of Broadcasters Hall of Fame in 2002.

Cormier implemented a new automation system for the station as well as extended the broadcast day to twenty-four hours. As a sign of the changing needs of advertisers and the change in the way consumers receive news and entertainment, WDEV added a digital services coordinator position. This position was tasked with creating digital content, managing social media and producing videos. The addition transformed WDEV from a radio station to a multimedia company.

The year 2019 marked the twenty-fifth anniversary of the weekly birding program *For the Birds*. What had begun with a listener asking for help identifying a little red bird developed into a weekly feature. The initial pairing of Anson Tebbetts and Bryan Pfeiffer lasted until 2010, at which point Chip Darmstadt from the North Branch Nature Center joined Tebbetts.

WDEV remains committed to continuing coverage in local communities and giving a voice to important issues affecting the region.

PART VI

COMMUNITY ORGANIZATIONS

1

COMMUNITY ACTION SERVICE TEAM (CAST)

Peter Plagge

CAST Inc., the acronym for the mouthful Community Action Service Team, grew naturally out of the small group of volunteers who were, at the time, running the Waterbury Area Food Shelf (Elaine, "Sis" Sabin and Adele Yandow) and the Waterbury Good Neighbor Fund. Our first meeting under that moniker was on March 24, 2003. Representatives from local churches, banks and businesses were present. Both of these entities were established sometime in the eighties with help from local pastors Reverend John Kirk and Reverend Paul Willard. CAST became a nonprofit organization in 2008 with the stated mission of being organized to assist lower income individuals in transitions and other difficult situations with such items as rent assistance, fuel oil, gasoline, groceries and the essentials of life; raising funds; and organizing volunteers to provide such assistance.

Our incorporation in 2008 was fortunate timing, as the work of the organization would increase thirtyfold in the year after the flood. Between August 2011 and January 2013, the fund alone (not including donations to the food shelf) totaled almost $400,000. Thanks to a dedicated group of volunteers from CAST (and of course, many others) who worked in the community providing food, clean-up assistance, housing coordination and checks to bridge the gap between insurance payouts and the immediate need to pay contractors, CAST became a vital component to Waterbury's recovery following Tropical Storm Irene.

Today we have one paid staff member, Danielle Kehlmann, who runs the Food Shelf, and a treasurer (Colin Pomer) to whom we pay a small stipend. The board meets once a month during regular, noncrisis days and more often when emergencies strike. In the first months of the COVID-19 lockdown, CAST Inc. received over $100,000 in donations and more food than we could stock.

The Food Shelf began serving food to food insecure Waterburians out of a closet in the Wesley United Methodist Church. The Food Shelf grew in usefulness to the people of the town of Waterbury, and it soon outgrew the closet and later a small side room in the church. In 1995, the Food Shelf moved across the street to the back room of the Methodist church parsonage and office space (57 South Main Street) where it is located as of this writing. When the Food Shelf moved to its current location, it served twenty-five households per month on average. By 2008, that number had increased fourfold, and we hired a part-time director, Cara Griswold. Now we serve over two hundred individuals per month and have a full-time director.

The Waterbury Good Neighbor Fund began as a way for local clergy to pool resources and have money to help out those facing small emergency financial needs. In the fall of 2001, the fund wrote one check each month at an average amount of $35. Three years later, donations to our neighbors in distress totaled $1,800 for the year. In the twelve months following Tropical Storm Irene and the devastating flooding of Waterbury and the Winooski River Valley, we received and distributed just over $385,000.

With a dedicated board of local volunteers, these two institutions will continue to serve the people of Waterbury, providing an unconditional leg up in times of need and continuing to address the problems of food insecurity.

2

BOY SCOUT TROOP 701

Nicole Fisher

Boy Scout Troop 701, part of the Green Mountain Council, has served the Waterbury area for over sixty years. The troop has stayed active even with the varying size of the group over the years. We were involved in many activities. We went winter camping and made snow shelters that we actually slept in. We participated in the Klondike Derby with other troops; it is a winter competition, like making a sled that we could pull the team on, snowshoe racing and other winter challenges. Annual summer camping at Mount Norris in Eden, Vermont, offered swimming, boating, gun safety, rock climbing, hiking, arts and crafts and fishing. Other opportunities included Spring Camporee located in different towns and "the Bogoree" at the Victory Bog in Victory, Vermont, in the fall. There, the featured activities and competitions taught strategizing and teamwork.

When there was a Cub Scout Pack, the troop helped with the Blue and Gold banquet, which celebrates the birth of scouting. As the Scouts came up the ranks, some went to National Youth Leadership Training at Camp Sunrise in Benson, Vermont, where they attended workshops to prepare them for being leaders in their troops. Sometimes we went on overnight backpacking trips and day hikes. The troop was treated to special Scout nights at the Mountaineers baseball game in Montpelier and the races at Thunder Road in Barre.

The highest rank in Boy Scouts is Eagle Scout. To earn that status, a Scout needs to earn at least twenty-one merit badges. Many Scouts have participated in Merit Badge Days that are sponsored by other troops or organizations to help them earn badges they need to become an Eagle Scout. A final project is chosen to accomplish and defend through an interview. The goal is for the Scout to be the project manager by making a plan, organizing workers, fundraising and soliciting donations. Fourteen in our troop have attained this rank. It is a true test in leadership.

In July 2017, a few lucky Scouts from Troop 701 spent two weeks in West Virginia at a National Jamboree with twenty-five-thousand-plus Scouts from across the country. Two busloads of boys from Vermont went, stopping to sightsee in Washington, D.C., for a couple of days on their way down. The event was held in the Summit Bechtel National Scout Reserve. It was an experience not to be forgotten.

We are thankful that the Waterbury American Legion Post 59 has been a great supporter of the troop. They paid the registration fees for each Scout and offered a place to hold meetings and scouting events. The Post offered their building for the troop's annual Italian Dinner fundraiser. In return, the Scouts helped with some of the Legion's activities: serving food for the annual Veterans Day dinner and taking part in the annual Flag Day burning of unserviceable flags ceremony. The troop often participated in the annual statewide Salute to Veterans parade.

Our community projects included Green-Up Day, helping with the sale of Christmas trees to benefit the Food Shelf, picking up trees after the holidays in Waterbury and Duxbury for the January bonfire and nighttime skating. During Winterfest one year, we were in charge of some of the activities for kids and also held a chess tournament that involved both kids and adults. Most recently, the Scouts were in charge of the bonfires after the River of Light parade and could be found helping out at the Memorial Day Ghost Walk.

While the current troop is small, leadership hopes to keep it going. The Scouts are only as good as the leadership. It takes time, enthusiasm, creativity and plenty of work to keep a group of boys interested and engaged. It looks like Troop 701 has indeed that.

3

GIRL SCOUT TROOP 30028

Kim Belongia

Waterbury Girl Scout Troop 30028 started in Waterbury in 2006 and operated until mid-2016. It was a small troop consisting of the same five girls for the entire ten years, with two other girls joining for several of those years. The troop started when the girls were young and continued until they graduated from Harwood. The troop focused predominantly on serving our communities of Waterbury and Duxbury, with some service activities reaching out to nearby Vermont towns and organizations.

The troop's largest community service project was the Pies for a Cause Project, a fundraiser the troop independently conceived and instituted. During September 2009, the local economy was failing, and many people were being laid off and struggling to meet their needs. The girls were motivated to do something to help.

At that time, our local food shelves were seeing ever increasing demand, so the troop decided they could contribute by raising money for them. Since it was almost Thanksgiving, they decided to embark on an adventure to sell holiday pies for hunger. The troop planned to bake apple and pumpkin pies, with proceeds going to our two local food shelves.

The Girl Scouts plunged right into their self-run fundraiser. They hung up flyers; submitted articles to local newspapers; took orders via email, phone and in person; and set up sale tables in local churches and on the sidewalk. They requested ingredients and supply donations from businesses. They picked many bushels of apples at local orchards. The girls spent long twelve-hour days preparing the pie filling: peeling, coring and slicing apples and adding spices to freeze for later use. They made and froze batches of piecrust dough. In November, the entire troop spent exhausting twelve-to-sixteen-hour days assembling and cooking the pies.

Each year, the troop made approximately 120 pies from scratch. Over the years, they donated $4,500 in total and secured an additional $1,500 in matching funds. After initially donating all proceeds to our local food shelves, they expanded their reach to the Good Neighbor Fund, a local emergency funding source for people in crisis.

In addition to Pies for a Cause, the troop volunteered to benefit the Waterbury Food Shelf in myriad ways: they unloaded and sold Christmas trees yearly at the Methodist church, created pottery bowls and served at the Empty Bowl fundraiser and worked at a local benefit clothing style swap.

Troop 30028 was also very active in the fight against cancer. For a number of years, the Scouts volunteered at the Nordic Relay for Life at Trapp Family Lodge, organizing and setting up the luminaria ceremony. They also cooked meals for families of cancer patients at Hope Lodge.

Troop 30028 was composed of Anna Belongia, Amber Proteau, Becca Russell, Madison D'Amico and Emma Jean for ten years. Lauren Harper and Abigail Willey joined for a number of those years.

4
REVITALIZING WATERBURY

Karen Nevin

Introduction

Revitalizing Waterbury (RW) was founded in 1991 by several Waterbury citizens committed to restoring the historic Stimson and Graves block, located downtown on Stowe Street. For the first seventeen years of operation, RW was an all-volunteer organization and today still depends heavily on the volunteer service of our community members. In 2006, RW played a lead role in Waterbury's successful application to become Vermont's twenty-second Designated Downtown, thus allowing property and business owners and the Town and Village of Waterbury to take advantage of special tax credit and grant opportunities. Following downtown designation, RW's work broadened beyond brick-and-mortar projects to a more holistic approach to revitalization that includes strengthening the local economy, encouraging physical improvements, developing special events and marketing the town as a destination for visitors.

After Tropical Storm Irene in 2011, ReBuild Waterbury formed as a major project of RW with the mission of assisting individuals and families in the area in need of assistance to rebuild their homes from the disastrous effects of the storm. ReBuild Waterbury achieved its million-dollar fundraising goal and coordinated a stunning fourteen-thousand-plus volunteer hours from November 2011 to April 2013. The project emerged as a leader and model for other recovery efforts around Vermont.

Through a 2015 agreement with the Town of Waterbury, RW hired an economic development director whose purpose is to encourage and support sustainable and responsible economic growth in Waterbury. In 2017, RW merged with the Waterbury Tourism Council to bring all promotional activities under one umbrella.

RW represents a creative community-based solution to solving challenges faced by small towns. The staff, volunteers and board offer a broad cross-section of expertise and contribute to long-term community planning and economic development, promoting Waterbury as a hub for artists, local food producers and restaurateurs, specialty food and drink purveyors and outdoor recreation enthusiasts.

Revitalizing Waterbury, a 501(c)(3) nonprofit organization, is a nationally accredited Main Street Program and serves as one of Vermont's twenty-three Designated Downtowns. Its mission is to strive to preserve, promote and enhance the economic, historic and social vitality of Waterbury, Vermont, for residents, businesses and visitors alike. RW seeks to make Waterbury a vibrant community that is inviting, safe, economically sound, lively and livable.

Projects and Accomplishments

Stimson and Graves Historic Restoration Project

Two dilapidated downtown buildings dodged the wrecking ball when RW formed in 1991 to renovate the historic Stimson and Graves building. The movement to restore the building and revitalize the downtown was dubbed "Miracles Happen." Located at the very center of Waterbury Village, near the corner of Main and Stowe Streets, the two cavernous three-story buildings had been vacant for more than twelve years until RW purchased the buildings for $196,300 and created affordable rental housing in the heart of downtown.

Partnering with Burlington-based Housing Vermont Inc., a statewide nonprofit that works with communities and the private sector, renovations began in 1991 and were completed in 1994. The project exemplified RW members' vision for the downtown and a vision for this building as an anchor facility that could become a focal point of the community and provide an identity, a sense of place and a visual community center for our town. RW's share of building ownership was transferred to Central Vermont Community

Land Trust (now Downstreet Housing & Community Development) in 2010, and the space currently houses the Waterbury Area Senior Center, retail space and twelve affordable apartments.

Waterbury Railroad Station

The Central Vermont Railroad Station sits in the center of Waterbury's village, at the head of Rusty Parker Memorial Park. Built in 1875, the station was the centerpiece of the downtown through the first half of the twentieth century but had deteriorated over the ensuing years. The interior had been totally reconfigured, losing its Italianate Victorian architectural detailing and ornamentation.

Revitalizing Waterbury began planning the restoration of the station in 1997. Major grant support came from the Great American Station Foundation, the Vermont Agency of Transportation and Green Mountain Coffee Roasters Foundation. A capital fundraising campaign was established and successfully met the goal of $1,200,000 through donations from the private sector and community members.

Keurig Green Mountain Inc. agreed to lease the station from RW and created a Visitor Center and Café that has become a first-class attraction and provided an economic boost to the downtown. Thousands of visitors from around the world have passed through the doors since it opened in October 2006. Unfortunately, the café closed in 2021 as a result of COVID-19.

The project was conceived to serve locals and travelers to the Waterbury region by providing a focal point for the downtown historic district; a transfer point to Amtrak and bus service; and a gateway to Pilgrim Park, Waterbury's leading industrial district, formerly the home of Keurig Dr Pepper's coffee brewing and manufacturing operations. The Waterbury Railroad Station restoration project is an example of successful collaboration among the nonprofit, governmental and business sectors while creating an informal hub for social activity.

Tropical Storm Irene Flood Recovery

On August 28 and 29, 2011, fed by nearly a foot of rainfall in less than twenty-four hours, the Winooski River overran its banks. Given the positioning of Waterbury's historic village alongside the Winooski River, the flooding was extensive. Over 220 residential, municipal and commercial buildings along Waterbury's Main Street corridor sustained significant damage, and over one thousand State of Vermont employees were displaced after the near-total destruction of the Waterbury State Office Complex.

ReBuild Waterbury, an offshoot of RW, was formed with the mission of assisting local individuals and families in need of assistance to rebuild their homes from the disastrous effects of Tropical Storm Irene. RW established the Business Flood Relief Fund in response to the serious damage to area businesses caused by Irene-related flooding. The application process was designed to allow RW to distribute the funds as expeditiously as possible and to provide support to all qualified applicants. While the majority of funds raised went to individual homeowners, $92,000 was disbursed to thirty-three local businesses. These grants were made possible by generous contributions to the fund from Keurig Green Mountain, National Life Group Charitable Foundation, the John and Barbara McLendon Foundation, Rise Up! Waterbury, Larkin Realty and Union Mutual Fire Insurance Company, along with a strong outpouring of support from individuals and businesses.

With the assistance of the Federal Emergency Management Agency's Long-Term Community Recovery (LTCR) team, Waterbury worked diligently through a seven-month process to identify the initiatives necessary to rebuild the community at every level. The process included a Waterbury Community Recovery Fair in February 2012 and a gathering of potential funding partners in attendance at the LTCR Plan unveiling in May 2012.

RW staff, board and volunteers assisted with many phases of the LTCR recovery effort and took direct responsibility for championing the first LTCR project: a Community Image Building and Retail Market Study Project. Arnett Muldrow and Associates were selected to assist Waterbury's community leaders in developing immediate and long-term strategies to achieve the goals of increased productivity, innovation, diversification, physical revitalization and job creation. RW raised $19,000 in grants from Keurig Green Mountain, Northfield Savings Bank, Ben & Jerry's Community Action Team, the Waterbury Tourism Council and the Town of Waterbury to support this project. The primary outcomes of this project consist of a Market and Retail Study Report and Waterbury Community Identity Guidelines.

Main Street Reconstruction

Though it had been in the works for over thirty years, the complete reconstruction of Main Street in downtown Waterbury finally began in 2019. RW, working with the Town's VTrans liaison and the State of Vermont, supported the businesses and community during construction including one-on-one meetings, email outreach, business meetings and promotional support. RW received a two-and-a-half-year grant from VTrans, through the town, of $162,500 for marketing and business support during the construction. RW created a construction-specific website and blog, held business support workshops and meetings and planned local shopping initiatives. RW's Marketing Committee supported the construction project with regional messaging directed at day-trippers.

Additional Accomplishments

- Waterbury Arts Fest: This annual community-centric event celebrates the arts, music and Waterbury's community. Currently in its nineteenth year, the event was taken over by RW around 2010 and turned into its largest annual fundraiser. Waterbury Arts Fest and the Friday Night Block Party, held in July each year, draw over four thousand visitors and raise $25,000 to support RW's work.
- *Discover Waterbury Guide*: Upon merging with the Waterbury Tourism Council, RW took over the printing of the *Discover Waterbury Guide*. Two editions have been printed (2016 and 2018), with twenty-five thousand copies distributed at state information centers, throughout the Mad River Valley and Stowe/Waterbury area.
- *The Waterbury Special*: RW and the Rotary Club of Waterbury partnered with other community organizations to envision, fundraise, commission and install a significant work of public art at the entrance to downtown Waterbury. *The Waterbury Special*, a low-relief aluminum sculpture created by Randolph artist Phillip Godenschwager, depicts historic buildings in the town of Waterbury as train cars. The train cars are pulled by a locomotive steam engine inspired by a drawing by the late Merrill Bennett, a locally known patient of the former

Waterbury Asylum. This sixty-foot-long, permanent public art piece was installed on September 9, 2018, on the one-hundred-plus-foot-long railroad bridge at the roundabout in Waterbury. It is the first piece of art ever to be installed on a New England Central Railroad working railroad bridge.

RW Programs and Initiatives

RW's staff, board and volunteers collaborate with other community nonprofits, government programs and statewide initiatives with compatible goals. Regular organizational activities include spearheading community-building events and "buy local" efforts; serving as the local conduit for the Vermont Small Business Development Center; and partnering with other organizations that honor local history, support local agriculture, outdoor recreation and arts, promote positive and diverse economic growth and make improvements to downtown infrastructure.

Revitalizing Waterbury's Standing Committees

Waterbury Area Development Committee | This committee identifies new market opportunities for the traditional commercial district, strengthens existing businesses and helps recruit new businesses. Projects include annual economic data collection and quarterly business mixers.

Design Committee | This committee plays a key role in shaping the physical image of Main Street as a place attractive to shoppers, investors, business owners and visitors. Projects include summer and fall flower plantings, holiday décor, banners, streetscape amenities and placemaking initiatives.

Marketing and Tourism Committee | Through events, marketing and promotional campaigns, this committee works to promote the downtown as the center of commerce, culture and community life for residents and visitors. Projects include the Waterbury Arts Fest and Friday Night Block Party and the Wrap It Up & Win Holiday shopping campaign.

Community Ambassadors | This group of volunteers ensures that seasonal visitors to Waterbury receive a warm welcome and helpful guidance on how to make the most of their visit to our community. Headquartered at the historic Waterbury Train Station, Community Ambassadors are passionate about local history, delight in meeting new people and love sharing information about the community.

STATION COMMITTEE | A committed group of volunteers monitors and resolves issues relating to the upkeep and maintenance of the Waterbury Train Station.

VOLUNTEER CORPS | The corps includes a growing list of volunteers who are interested in supporting RW with time and talent. Corps members receive emails when help is needed. Projects may include planting barrels, working at the Waterbury Arts Fest and helping in the office.

REVITALIZING WATERBURY AND WATERBURY'S FUTURE

After thirty years, Revitalizing Waterbury is poised to serve Waterbury and its community for years to come. Our mission continues to guide the work of the organization, ensuring that our businesses remain strong, our streets welcoming and our lives as a community joyous. Through a strong strategic planning process, RW's board of directors maintains a focus on economic development, partnering with local organizations and nonprofits, promoting our town as a premier destination for visitors, engaging and recognizing our volunteers and maintaining fiscal responsibility and sustainability. Through this lens, we will look into the future to support diversity and inclusion in our work and in our community.

5

ROTARY CLUB OF WATERBURY

Allyn Lewis

The Waterbury Rotary Club (the Club) began meeting as a group of thirty-nine local businessmen in November 1936 and received its charter on December 7, 1936, under then Rotary International (RI) District No. 4075 (now No. 7850 serving parts of Vermont, New Hampshire and Quebec, Canada) and celebrated its Charter Night on February 9, 1937. The Club ushered in the twenty-first century under the leadership of Club presidents William C. Riegel (principal of Waterbury's Thatcher Brook Primary School) and Jeff Larkin (owner of Arvad's Restaurant). By then, meetings were held as breakfasts on Tuesdays at 7:15 a.m. at the Holiday Inn on Blush Hill. In 2002, the Club began a lasting relationship with the Waterbury Senior Center and met there until recently, when the coronavirus pandemic forced a change to virtual meetings.

The Club maintained its four avenues of service with committees for each chaired by members: club service, vocational service, community service and international service. Each year the Club identifies fundraising initiatives to support local and international projects, community events, student scholarships and achievement recognition. Over the past twenty years, the Club held a variety of raffles and fundraisers. One of the largest fundraising events has been the local Home, Garden and Recreation Show held in the spring. An Independence Day event named Not Quite Independence Day (NQID) is hosted by the Rotary. This annual fundraising celebration includes carnival rides and games for families, band concerts and, for a few years, a nationally sanctioned BBQ competition. This event drew competitors from Vermont, New York and other New England states. In February each year, the Club sponsors a "Pie for Breakfast" fundraiser, with funds supporting RI's student exchange program. This program gives two to five local students the opportunity to live abroad for a year, learn another language and complete their academic year in another country.

The Club has supported a number of programs and the academic achievement of local students in grades four through twelve. Each year on Arbor Day, the Club provides trees, which are then ceremonially planted at the Thatcher Brook, Crossett Brook and Moretown Schools. The Club also sponsored a Renaissance Program for the Crossett Brook Middle School, Harwood Middle School and Harwood Union High School. This program began in 1998 and ran for eighteen years. It recognized students' academic achievement, and with this acknowledgement, students were awarded certificates, gifts and discount purchases throughout the community. Students with exceptional academic achievements met with local business owners for a behind the scenes introduction to running a successful business.

Programs at the high school level supported by the Rotary include the Interact Club at Harwood. This club gives student members the opportunity to learn about the Rotary organization and how local and international volunteer service can benefit society. The Interact Club members select worthy projects and then raise funds through various means, including providing their labor for a fee or completing odd jobs. The Rotary also awards two or three high school seniors scholarships for higher education. In recent years, students have been awarded laptop computers in lieu of cash. Additionally, the Club has awarded "tools of the trade" to a graduating senior at the Spaulding Trade School.

The calendar propels the Club's community service initiatives beginning in January with the planning for the Home, Garden and Recreation Show, which occurs in March, with as many as seventy booths filling the gym, cafeteria and hallways of Crossett Brook Middle School. This show provides local merchants the opportunity to display and sell their merchandise. Nonprofits are well represented with organizational programs and information. This show often draws up to one thousand visitors.

April's warmer weather sees the Rotary sponsoring an Easter parade and egg hunt at the Pilgrim Park fields. May brings final planning for the annual Rotary Club Concerts in the Park summer program, which begins in early June and runs through the end of August. By the fall of

2020, the Club had recorded thirty-eight consecutive seasons of providing music entertainment; however, due to the COVID-19 pandemic, the Club created a Concert in the Parking Lot series of four concerts, which were quite successful. The Club maintains and performs spring clean-up at the Rusty Parker Park facilities, including the Rotary-built gazebo and bandstand. The Club is also responsible for many improvements to the park, which are completed with volunteer labor and funded by the Club.

October celebrates harvest with the Search for Sunzilla contest, which honors the tallest, widest and heaviest sunflower as well as the longest and heaviest zucchini. Kids and their parents eagerly participate, with some great results from their gardens. Toward the end of October, the Rotary hosts a Halloween Haunted Forest. Over the past twenty years, the Club's Halloween festivity grew from children parading around in costumes at Thatcher Brook Primary School to the Rotary crew managing a Haunted House, first in the park bandstand and then at the Thatcher Brook School stage in the gym, to finally a Haunted Forest held at Thatcher Brook Primary School. October is also the month when preparations are made for decorating the Rusty Parker Park gazebo and the tree of lights, which is erected on the hill above Thatcher Brook Primary School to welcome students, local travelers and visitors home for the holidays.

For the last few years, the Club has organized the annual turkey drive in November, gathering whole turkeys and hams from local contributors for distribution to the Waterbury Food Shelf.

When it is time for Santa to visit Waterbury in December, he arrives with Mrs. Santa to Rusty Parker Park. For many years, Santa and Mrs. Santa arrived at the Rusty Parker Park sitting on their sleigh; here they listened to children's wishes for presents under the tree while Club members handed out hot chocolate and roasted chestnut and delivered small gifts for the children. Free horse-drawn sleigh and wagon rides for family and friends were a tradition during this event, and on occasion, there was a winter firework display. When the weather was nasty or too cold, this event moved inside to the Waterbury Senior Center.

A few other community service projects should be highlighted before closing out the last twenty years. Rotary partnered with Revitalizing Waterbury and the community to commission *The Waterbury Special* (a train sculpture), donated a computer to the town library and installed a water fountain at the elementary school playground. Additionally, the Club is now in the process of planning and permitting a roller skate and skateboard park to be built in the community. Over the years, the Club has also made significant cash contributions to the Waterbury Food Shelf and Waterbury Senior Center and many smaller monetary contributions to other nonprofits in the surrounding area. The Waterbury Rotary Club is one of the most active Rotary Clubs within the RI District No. 7850. Its membership is diverse, and the members' classifications span a broad range of retail, restaurant, service, municipal and professional fields of expertise.

6

WATERBURY AREA ANTI-RACISM COALITION

Life LeGeros

The Waterbury Area Anti-Racism Coalition (WAARC) grew out of a multiracial, multigenerational group of community members who gathered to organize the Waterbury Rally Against Racism on June 14, 2020, in response to the powerful words of Damien Garcia, an eighth grader from Waterbury. Damien had spoken about the racism he had experienced in our community at a rally at the Vermont State House the week prior.

Following the rally, many of the organizers and newly engaged community members committed to continuing as WAARC. WAARC holds monthly meetings for members, a structure that drives strategic action. WAARC includes a steering team in addition to multiple specialized teams comprising a mural team, an education team and an outreach team. All positions are filled on a voluntary basis, and all teams, including the steering team, are open to all members.

In its first year, WAARC held ongoing conversations with the Waterbury Selectboard about racism and antiracism. This resulted in hanging a Black Lives Matter (BLM) banner at the town office and adopting a statement of inclusion in 2020. There have been numerous additional actions: the design and distribution of a BLM yard sign, securing a fiscal sponsor, launching a website, raising thousands of dollars from local businesses, holding candidate forums for select and school boards that centered on antiracism and equity, held space for community members to process traumatic collective events such as the Capitol insurrection and cosponsoring with the Waterbury

Public Library and student leaders from Harwood Union High School a community conversation considering the elementary school was named after a slaveholder, which led to the school board voting unanimously to change the school's name.

Individuals who join WAARC must sign an agreement that speaks to various aspects of WAARC's principles. These include:

- Prioritizing voices and leadership of members of color. We acknowledge that members who are Black, Indigenous and people of color have acute insight into the mechanisms of racism and its impacts and strategies for making our community more antiracist.
- Empowering students and families of color. We want to include all members of our community and beyond, but we will intentionally center and serve community members of color.
- Continuous learning and growth. In addition to listening to and learning from members of color during our meetings, we are committed to ongoing collaborative and individual study of racism, its impacts and antiracist concepts and strategies.
- Focus on impact. We seek to help make substantial change in our community and to operate organizationally in a way that minimizes the reproduction of racist structures and relationships. Our processes for working together will assume that the dynamics of white dominant culture are likely to cause harm to our members of color, and we will seek to minimize this harm and to repair it when it happens.

WAARC's mission is to help create a community where every person can fully experience freedom, belonging and daily love. Its members are committed to challenging racism at all levels, including interpersonal racism (both conscious and unconscious acts) and systemic racism (our local institutions and policies). Together they work toward a better future through education, advocacy and activism.

7
WATERBURY AREA SENIOR CENTER

Vicki Brooker

The Waterbury Area Senior Center's purpose is to enrich the lives of older persons by providing services and activities that sharpen their minds, improve their physical and emotional health and help keep them active, independent and involved in life.

The Waterbury Senior Citizens Club was formed by nine ladies at the home of Ethel Colby in 1964. The charter was received in 1965. For a time, the Club met at the American Legion until it was determined they needed a larger space for on-site cooking. Saint Leo's Hall at Saint Andrew Catholic Church provided that space from 1983 to 1989. From the beginning, the seniors dreamed of a site that they could claim as their own. That dream came true when the Senior Citizens Club became one of the first tenants in the renovated Stimson and Graves building on Stowe Street; they have continued to reside in this building as the Waterbury Area Senior Center ever since.

Isabel Boyce was hired to serve as the executive director and remained in that role until 2000. Since 2000, the center has had several executive directors, including Susan Ellsasser, Wallie Roberts, Karol Smith and Jodi LaVanway. Vicki Brooker was hired to be the executive director in 2020.

To better serve the community and to raise money, the Senior Center joined the Meals on Wheels of America program, which has proven to be a vital community service since it began in 2008. Until the onset of the coronavirus, the center was open for the community to enjoy congregate meals.

In the past twenty years, the Senior Center has provided programs that included low-impact exercise classes; foot clinics; computer classes; local history presentations; and games such as bingo, cribbage, poker, canasta and the popular Mexico train dominoes. With the support of AARP, yearly safe driving classes and tax return assistance have been available.

The Senior Center has a reputation for offering delicious food and, for a time, provided a catering service to raise extra funds. Throughout the past twenty years, the center has provided lunch at town meetings, Mother's Day brunches, harvest dinners, hunters' breakfasts and an annual Christmas cookie and chocolate sale. In 2020, the Senior Center prepared approximately 520 meals each week for community delivery.

8
WATERBURY HISTORICAL SOCIETY

Chris Palermo

On April 24, 1957, the newly formed Waterbury Historical Society met in the museum rooms at the Waterbury Public Library. The purpose, or mission statement, was to collect and preserve the papers, photos and artifacts pertaining to the town of Waterbury.

In the ensuing sixty-three years, the Waterbury Historical Society through its membership, community and boards of directors has collected extensive and varied artifacts that piece together our community's life story spanning centuries. Were it not for the twenty-four founding members, our community would not have the privilege of owning and sharing its history.

The Waterbury Historical Society's humble beginning was founded upstairs in the Waterbury Village Public Library, located at 28 North Main Street in the former Dr. Henry Janes home. Piece by piece, displays were created, and the historical society took root. Over the ensuing years, board members and volunteers proudly nurtured the growing collection of artifacts. It is with great appreciation to the library trustees for allowing the historical society to use the upstairs of the main house for a museum and storage. Not much changed in terms of the infrastructure of the building for decades: the parquet floor, fluorescent lights and green velvet curtain that was the "security door" for archive storage. But the heart and soul of the society were alive and thriving.

At the center of this movement, the proverbial "hub around which the spokes revolved," was Linda Kaiser. To say that the historical society would not be where it is today without her dedication, knowledge and hard work would be a vast understatement. Her decades of service as archivist, collector, meticulous recordkeeper and taskmaster single-handedly kept the society together and moving forward with acquisitions and their preservation.

As the Waterbury Town and Village, along with the public library, began contemplating a new municipal complex to house all municipal functions, the historical society requested to be a part of the conversation and plan. It was simple—without the ability to be included, the society could little afford to go it alone. Fortunately, as the planners saw the value in collecting, preserving and sharing Waterbury's rich history, the historical society was brought into the fold as a part of the new proposed facility. Looking first at buildings located at the state complex, the community ultimately decided on renovating and adding on to the former Dr. Janes home. As part of the negotiations for our space within the facility, the historical society was required to raise $100,000 as a contribution to the project. This secured the historical society a lease agreement for ninety-nine years that includes increased display space, heat, air conditioning, power and janitorial service. In addition, it was necessary to raise an $80,000 for displays, secure storage cabinets, lighting, office equipment and a security system. In partnership with the community, through the annual support of tax dollars, the society can have a paid intern to enter data and scan information to the PastPerfect program, which is specifically designed for cataloging and organizing historic collections. All of this was accomplished by the stewardship of the board of directors, which included Chris Palermo, Theresa Wood, Paul and Jane Willard, Jan Gendreau, David Luce, Jack Carter and archivist Linda Kaiser.

Today, the historical society is proud to be a part of the new Waterbury Municipal Center at 28 North Main Street, located on the first and second floors of the original Dr. Henry Janes home. As we have moved into the twenty-first century bringing our history forward, we now have our collection digitally available through the PastPerfect program, display space has expanded into the historic train station and outreach through education programs involve the community and schools, along with special projects like the award-winning series *Waterbury Women—Stories and Inspiration*.

The Waterbury Historical Society is open to the public five days a week. Please take some time to visit, bring your family and explore all that our rich history has to offer.

9

WATERBURY PUBLIC LIBRARY

Jill Chase

It was the best of times, it was the worst of times…
—Charles Dickens, A Tale of Two Cities

The twenty years between 2000 and 2020 were tumultuous ones for Waterbury. Failures, successes, feuds, alliances and a devastating flood showed how powerfully a town could pull together. Those years were no less challenging for the library.

For decades, there were two libraries, one in the Seminary Building in Waterbury Center and the other in Dr. Janes's home on Main Street in the village. By 2000, these two had been joined into one library system for the town with one board of commissioners. Donna Boring was the director, headquartered in the village, with Sue Sayah the librarian in the Center. Business was brisk, and both libraries had been in their buildings, well loved by residents, for over one hundred years. While fond memories remained, the structures were aging and getting crowded. Citizens wanted books, audiobooks, movies, space for programs and meetings for children and adults, all of which were hard to squeeze in.

While the commissioners were working on ways to expand the village location, big changes were coming to the Center. The Seminary Building, which housed the library, was sold to the Central Vermont Community Land Trust. The old school was to be renovated into affordable apartments with space reserved for the library.

In December, Mary Kasamatsu replaced Donna Boring as the new library director, and she had to hit the ground running. There was planning and implementing the move of the Center library in 2001. The downsized collection had to be incorporated into the village location or stored away. There wasn't room for the Center staff and the village staff to work at the same time in the tight quarters, so library hours were expanded to provide hours for members of both staffs. Residents of Waterbury thereby benefited by having greater access to their library than many other communities of similar size.

At the same time, the library was coming to terms with joining the world of automation. Card catalogues all over the country were falling to online catalogues and patron systems that could keep track and track down materials of all sorts. Thanks to a major improvement grant from the Vermont Public Library Foundation, funded by the Freeman Foundation, Waterbury was able to tackle the job. A system had to be chosen, catalogue cards converted to computer records and barcodes applied to books and other library materials and scanned into the system. Paper forms fell to automated searches for interlibrary loans. And computers became available. Library staff and volunteers had to learn to use the new software to perform work that had always used pencil and paper technology. And they had to come up to speed quickly so they could help patrons search for materials, find information on the internet and do all of the things they wanted to do with the new technology. The public computers were instantly popular for emailing, job hunting, submitting applications, filing unemployment claims, ordering goods, taking classes and tests and just exploring the world wide web.

The work on the Center library quarters was completed in the summer of 2002. Volunteers helped hang shelves and unpack boxes in the renovated space, and the library reopened in the fall. However, things had changed. Two large structural pillars now broke up the open program space, making it harder to accommodate programs or group meetings. And the community had gotten used to visiting the village library, finding it easy to stop by when they had errands downstreet, especially with the expanded hours. This had a devastating effect on the usage of the Center library, even with its own collection largely restored. By the fall of 2005, the beautifully renovated library was seeing only a handful of visitors each week. Public meetings ensued as to what should be done, and emotions ran high, but in the end, the library commissioners decided it would make better economic sense to close the Center library and concentrate their funds in the village location. The Select Board concurred, and the Center branch closed at the end of 2005.

Meanwhile, in the village, the automation process was completed, and the Waterbury Public Library had created a webpage. The bookmobile was providing services in summer, and there were more programs for children and adults than ever, due partly to the introduction of a program coordinator. Some of these programs were funded by the efforts of the Friends of the Library, an energetic group of volunteers who run book sales, support library programs and provide books for newborn babies (as well as information about library and town services for families with children) in Waterbury and Duxbury. Local businesses and groups, like the Rotary, often stepped in with support. And many residents gladly volunteered their services in a number of ways.

This includes the commissioners and those who were still working hard on finding a solution to the problem of the village building. By 2004, the commissioners turned their attention to exploring options for expanding the library beyond the Janes house. To extend the existing building, three and a half acres of land designated as recreational would have to be swapped for municipally owned land elsewhere that could be used for recreation. Negotiations to find land that would appease government regulations as well as the people of Waterbury commenced in 2005. Adding on to the existing building would affect the public gardens, though these did not technically fall under recreational guidelines. Many longtime gardeners, not to mention residents along Winooski Street, were not happy with this proposal, and they and others showed their displeasure at the 2006 village and town meetings when the proposal that the village transfer a parcel of land to the town was defeated.

Things kept moving along at the library. Digital services were starting to be added in 2008 with access to Recorded Books and an online program where one could learn dozens of languages. The librarians and visitors made the best of the crowded space with no barrier-free access. And the notorious bump at the end of the driveway just kept growing, taking out tires and suspension systems.

Then, in 2011, came Irene. The storm caused flooding throughout downtown Waterbury. The municipal offices were ruined; people's basements were filled with mud and contaminated with oil from their fuel tanks. The state offices were inundated up to the second floor, and all the employees had to be relocated to other sites around Vermont.

The Select Board leaped into action supported by the village trustees, and the townspeople responded immediately as wholehearted volunteers.

Though the library also had three feet of basement flooding, which damaged the furnace, it still had electricity. Once things were cleaned up and good to go, the library opened its doors for people who needed a place to get information, have internet access and just rest in a calm place when their own homes were complete wrecks.

When FEMA arrived, beyond immediate disaster assistance, it facilitated committees of Waterbury residents to work on essential projects from new community buildings to flood mitigation and disaster preparedness. These committees met all winter long, coming up with various suggestions on which voters could provide feedback at town meeting. The municipal office and library construction came out as the number one concern.

New building committees were formed of the Select Board, village trustees, library commissioners and Waterbury residents. They were tasked with finding a location, selecting a design and presenting a bond for a vote. The State Complex was seriously considered but in the end proved unfeasible. The area behind the old library was ultimately chosen as the best solution, though technicalities and opposition had to be overcome. The plan was to refurbish the Janes house to accommodate some town office space as well as the Waterbury Historical Society. Though the society had spent decades on the second floor above the library, the remodeling would correct structural issues and give them a museum show room on the first floor as well. The remaining municipal offices with a community room would extend from there with the two-story library on the end.

Bonds fail easily in hard times, and the library and the historical society wanted to do what they could to ensure success. Rather than competing against each other for donations, they worked collaboratively. They pledged funds to be raised through a public appeal to supplement the construction costs. The Friends of the Library joined in, and Waterbury citizens responded with donations above the goals that had been set. The bond passed at town meeting in 2014 and survived a rescission effort by a wide margin; the people were behind this.

By the winter of 2015, it was time for the library to pack up and move once more. This time, it relocated to 30 Foundry Street to spend the months during construction. Amazing volunteers stepped up to the plate, packing and lugging boxes, filling cars and a flatbed truck loaned for the occasion. The driver of that particular rig spent a couple of days loading and unloading. Then volunteers helped the staff set it up at the other end. (The library really couldn't have functioned as it has all these years without all the generous volunteers who helped out in so many ways. They are indeed too numerous to list but heartily appreciated.) Everyone adapted to the space but looked forward to the last move, even when it meant doing things all over again.

Once the Janes building was empty, construction could begin in the spring of 2015. Vermont Integrated Architects of Middlebury was chosen as the designer and ReArch of South Burlington the builder. A large cherry tree that stood at the far end of the Janes house had to be taken down for construction, but the wood was turned into a sleek circulation desk and architectural accents by Stark Mountain Woodworking, and donation benches were crafted by Ben Keaton. Shelving was constructed by Vermont Correctional Industries. A warm and whimsical mural was painted by Sarah-Lee Terrat to acknowledge many who had contributed during fundraising. It features Dr. Janes, his wife and a tree with branches and fruit that represents all the wonderful people of Waterbury who saw this project through. The new building opened in February 2016.

At the annual Vermont Library Conference in 2017, Harriet Grenier (sixteen years as library commissioner) and Margaret Luce (commissioner for over thirty years) were chosen as Vermont's Library Trustees of the Year. It was unusual to give this award to two commissioners, but the long-term dedication and unflagging efforts by both of these women to see a new library built deserved recognition.

Though the old quarters had been cozy and familiar, the new library is open to light and views of Harvey's Hill, Blush Hill and vistas heading north. A flower and a word garden bloom next to the parking area. The program room offers workshops on mushrooms, astronomy, trout fishing and fly-tying, yoga, tai chi and qigong, writing, ukulele and craft and educational programs for young and old. The two small study rooms accommodate tutors, small business owners and students. In 2013, Waterbury Public Library helped create the Catamount consortium of libraries from across the state, which combined all their separate catalogues into one. Patrons could now choose items to borrow from any of these libraries, and when the state began a courier service, the new library office could accommodate the bins needed to shuttle the items back and forth.

Mary Kasamatsu, who managed to provide continued library service while planning and moving to a new building, retired in the fall of 2018. Almy Landauer was chosen as her successor and from early spring of 2020 has had to pilot the library through COVID-19. As virus surges closed the library's doors for browsing, physical items were harder to supply. Though patrons had already been able to connect from home, or wherever they might be, to listen to or read books, magazines, watch movies, shows and even concerts, suddenly the use of online resources soared. The new director has promoted more online programming to fill the gaps when in-person story times and workshops have been impossible.

It will always be the best of times, the worst of times. But as they say, libraries will get you through times of no money better than money will get you through times of no libraries. May this public haven, one of the few places left that welcomes all and offers so much, prosper and flourish for decades to come.

PART VII

EDUCATION

1

CHANGES IN EDUCATION

Theresa A.M. Wood

Waterbury and Duxbury—A New Partnership

As the turn of the century approached, there were big changes in store for education in Waterbury and for the neighboring community of Duxbury. Waterbury and Duxbury have had a long tradition of shared educational services dating back to the days when Waterbury had its own high school. At that time, Duxbury students attended high school with their Waterbury friends and neighbors at the school buildings on Stowe Street in Waterbury. And in 1967, when Harwood Union High School opened, both towns sent their seventh through twelfth graders to the new school.

In the spring of 1993, preliminary discussions began between the Duxbury School Board and the Waterbury School Board to investigate interest in pursuing a joint project between the two communities. Prior to that, the Duxbury School Board had attempted on two different occasions (in March 1989 and again in September 1989) to pursue building a new elementary school on the site of the old State Farm in Duxbury. Negotiations for a new Duxbury Elementary School hit a snag when the Agency of Agriculture withdrew its support for the project because of objections from the farmer who was leasing the land. In April 1989, the legislature ultimately did pass a bill that authorized the sale of the farmland to the Town of Duxbury. The bill number authorizing the sale was S.45, an interesting coincidence since the union school district between Waterbury and Duxbury was ultimately given the designation of Union 45, or U-45 as some called it.

The Department of Education made it clear to Duxbury that its elementary school was never going to be able to meet the public school approval minimum standards for a school facility. It was evident that library, health, physical education, guidance and arts programs were severely limited in the existing building and that Duxbury must develop a plan to stop using that facility.

While Duxbury was investigating options, Waterbury was faced with a school facility that was not meeting the needs of a growing student population. At the same time, the Washington West Supervisory Union was discussing the potential for a separate middle school to serve the whole district. Ultimately, nothing materialized with that discussion.

During the summer and fall of 1993, an independent assessment was commissioned from the New England School Development Council and the Waterbury and Duxbury School Boards continued discussions regarding a potential merger, working closely with the Department of Education. The Town of Moretown participated in some of these discussions but ultimately declined to participate in the proposed new district. In January 1994, the communities of Duxbury and Waterbury each voted to support a planning committee. However, a budget to support the planning failed. Volunteers on the planning committee[1] worked nonetheless from February to April 1994 to develop the report required by statute, and in April 1994, the planning report was submitted to the Department of Education and State Board of Education outlining what a merged district would look like. By June 1994, the State Board of Education had approved the formation of the new union school district.

In the summer of 1994, the commissioner of education and the secretary of state certified the new Waterbury-Duxbury Union School District No. 45. The new school district would comprise the buildings located on Stowe Street in Waterbury (called Waterbury Elementary School at the time) and a new middle school campus located at the former State Farm in Duxbury.[2] But now the voters needed to weigh in.

In June 1994, each town, Waterbury and Duxbury, voted to support the planning committee report—the affirmative vote created the Union

1. The planning committee consisted of representatives from Duxbury and Waterbury as follows: Linda Aldrich, Cathy Buck, Ed Finn, Ron Fox, Robert Magee Jr., Beth Ann Maier, George Pierce, Mary Lou Shane, Otho Thompson (chair), Henry Wall and Theresa Wood.

2. Several sites were evaluated for the location of the new middle school, including the location of the land where the Country Club of Vermont is located in Waterbury. The old State Farm site in Duxbury was chosen for a variety of reasons, including cost, flow of transportation from the primary school to Harwood Union High School and to enable Duxbury residents to have a school facility close to their former Duxbury Elementary School to continue a sense of community.

School District No. 45, but again voters failed to approve any planning funds. In September 1994, the first organizing meeting of Union No. 45 was held and a board of directors was elected.

With the State Board of Education approval and the approval of both Duxbury and Waterbury residents, what more could be needed? Well, Waterbury and Duxbury were part of the Harwood Union School District for their seventh and eighth graders, as well as high school students. In order to make the new Union No. 45 both programmatically and financially feasible, the seventh and eighth graders would need to be part of the newly formed school district. Thus, a vote was required in all six towns of the Harwood Union School District (Duxbury, Fayston, Moretown, Waitsfield, Warren and Waterbury) to allow the Waterbury and Duxbury seventh and eighth graders to leave the Harwood Union School District. That vote needed to pass in each town separately; there were no comingled votes. Amazingly enough, all six towns voted to allow the students to leave the Harwood Union School District. It should be noted that at the same time this was taking place, the Harwood Union School Board was considering a renovation bond of its own. Perhaps the desire to have more space at the Harwood campus influenced the outcome of the affirmative vote? Ultimately, a major renovation bond also passed to upgrade the Harwood campus.

From October 1994 to October 1995, the newly elected Union No. 45 School Board worked to develop a mission and philosophy for the new school district. The board interviewed architects, ultimately selecting the firm of Banwell, White, Arnold, Hemberger and Partners Inc. to design the new middle school. The board prepared cost and enrollment estimates and conducted numerous informational meetings in the community and in community members' homes. This personal approach allowed people to ask questions and feel more comfortable with the proposal, which in the end would build a new middle school, increase educational opportunities and cost less than what they were already paying. It almost seemed impossible, but it was proven true.

In October 1995, Duxbury and Waterbury each held a vote to build the new middle school. The bond vote passed by more than a 2:1 margin. The vision of a new merged school district was now becoming a reality, but there were still many hurdles to overcome, not the least of which was the acquisition of the State Farm land, several more votes and receiving state aid for school construction.[3]

Negotiations continued with the legislature for Duxbury to purchase the State Farm land. What was once going to be deeded to the town for a nominal

3. Because Duxbury and Waterbury were merging two school districts and forming one, state aid for construction was 50 percent of eligible costs, higher than it would have otherwise been at 30 percent.

amount now had a price tag of $126,000. That figure, coupled with a 20 percent buy-in interest in the Waterbury Elementary School for $644,000, was ultimately approved by Duxbury voters in December 1995. The $644,000 buy-in was turned over by the school district to the Town of Waterbury to create a tax stabilization fund that as of 2021 continues to serve that purpose.

From October 1995 through August 1996, the school board worked with the Washington West superintendent and its architects to finalize the middle school design, arrange for additional site analyses of soils, prepare bid specifications and prepare numerous permit applications. In the summer of 1996, the sale of the State Farm land was finalized, and the first two educational leaders (aka principals) were chosen. Bid openings for the construction of the middle school and a groundbreaking ceremony occurred. Wright and Morrissey was selected to build the new middle school, and construction was underway.

Creating a new school district and constructing a new school were just the beginning. During the year of construction, the team was not only working on guiding the new school construction, but the curriculum was finalized, staff were interviewed and hired, transition plans for students returning from Harwood Union happened, multiple community and staff meetings occurred and school names were chosen as well. The Waterbury Elementary School was named the Thatcher Brook Primary School, and the middle school in Duxbury was named Crossett Brook Middle School. The names were chosen to acknowledge brooks in the area. A closing community picnic was planned for Duxbury Elementary School. The educational leaders were not only preparing for the new school district but also simultaneously running the existing two elementary schools.

On Town Meeting Day in March 1997, the first operating budget of the Waterbury-Duxbury School District was approved by voters. The school board delivered a budget that was $40,410 *less than* the budget it had estimated during the bond vote process. The voters appreciated the board's efforts and approved the first budget of the Waterbury-Duxbury School District totaling $4.7 million for 833 students at an average cost per student of $5,586.

On July 1, 1997, the Waterbury-Duxbury School District and its accompanying board of school directors[4] officially took over school operations

---

4. The Waterbury-Duxbury School Board that shepherded the process from conception to operation was composed of Bob Minter, Laurel Scannell, Cindy Senning, Henry Wall and Theresa Wood (chairperson). Jeffrey Kilgore was initially on the board for a brief time. Bill Riegel, former principal at Waterbury Elementary School and superintendent of Washington West Supervisory Union, along with Ken Page, final Duxbury Elementary principal and first Crossett Brook Middle School education leader, were integral to the planning process.

from the Duxbury School Board and the Waterbury School Board. While these two school boards no longer had responsibility for running schools, they remained "on the books" to participate in Washington West Supervisory Union governance and to receive state aid on behalf of each town.

August 27, 1997, just a year after construction commenced, marked the first day of school for students at Thatcher Brook Primary School in Waterbury and Crossett Brook Middle School in Duxbury. The school construction project and all the planning to combine school districts had become reality. The construction project was accomplished on budget ($6.5 million in construction and $.4 million in fit up) and on time. On September 3, 1997, both schools were dedicated with ceremonies, including an appearance from Governor Howard Dean.

Renovations to Thatcher Brook Primary School

The Waterbury-Duxbury School Board did not rest with the creation of the new school district and construction of the new middle school. At the same time construction was finishing up on the new middle school, initial improvements to Thatcher Brook Primary School were also being completed by E.F. Wall. These renovations included improvements to ventilation, new roofs, asbestos abatement, electrical improvements, a new heating plant and computer networking at a cost of $838,000.

After a brief respite, the school board planned for more major renovations to Thatcher Brook Primary School for the district's youngest students. Two bond votes to construct a new building addition behind the existing center building failed twice, once in 2002 and again in 2003. The third proposal to renovate the existing structures, including completing access between buildings on all three levels, completely renovating the lower level for classrooms, addressing accessibility for people with mobility issues and improving bus drop off and parking was approved by voters in June 2005. The total cost of the project was $7.8 million, with the state paying 30 percent. Renovating the one-hundred-plus-year-old historic building wasn't without its controversy. Some people believed the buildings should be torn down and new ones constructed. However, in the end, preserving the history and solid construction of the historic school won out, but not without another vote. In August 2005, after receiving a petition to rescind the June vote, voters again approved the construction project by defeating the motion to rescind.

Scott and Partners were chosen as the architects and DEW Construction received the bid to complete the work. From 2005 to 2007, construction was accomplished in phases while school functions were still being carried out.

Classrooms moved and then moved again, and despite the stress of teaching in a building under construction, staff remained flexible and upbeat awaiting the final product. The "new" school opened in the fall of 2007 with a brief ribbon-cutting ceremony.

More Mergers

In 2015, the Vermont legislature passed Act 46 in an attempt to streamline governance and address rising education costs and lack of equity in access to educational services and support. The act provided incentives through reduced property taxes for a brief period to school districts that voted to merge voluntarily. Each of the six towns in the Washington West Supervisory Union voted to merge into one unified union; hence the Harwood Unified Union School District was formed and began operation as of July 1, 2017. The Waterbury-Duxbury School Board and all of the other school boards in the supervisory union were abandoned in favor of one unified school board to operate all of the elementary schools in Waterbury, Moretown, Fayston, Warren and Waitsfield; the middle schools in Duxbury and at Harwood; and the Harwood Union High School. The Articles of Agreement passed by voters called for a fourteen-member school board with weighted votes. Waterbury has four members with a weight of 39.4 percent of the votes on the board. When combined with Duxbury's two members and weight of 10.4 percent, the previous communities that were members of the Waterbury-Duxbury School District total nearly half of the voting weight on the school board at 49.8 percent.

Education structure, governance and financing have long been debated in Vermont, and it is likely that will continue into the future. Proposals for shifting from a primarily property tax–based system to an income tax–based system continue to crop up. One thing is for certain, for as long as there are children to educate, there will be debates about how to pay for it.

2
THE CHILDREN'S ROOM

Melissa Phillips, adapted by Naomi Alfini

The Children's Room, officially named the Early Education Resource Center of Waterbury, first opened its doors on February 1, 1984, with the mission of "serving all families with young children in the Waterbury and Duxbury communities by providing information which increases knowledge of parenting and caregiving skills, and by offering support to parents and caregivers of young children."

In its thirty-five years, the Children's Room has expanded its reach and served thousands of young children and their caregivers of the greater surrounding area, from Middlesex to Fayston and Stowe to Barre. Its mission and goals have also evolved. Under the direction of Anne Latulippe, who served as board chair and then coordinator from 2004 to 2018, the room shifted focus from primarily supporting caregivers and combating the social isolation that can come from living in a rural area with young children to supporting young children and their families and caregivers by providing opportunities for playing, learning and gathering with other community members, "with the goal of promoting children's intellectual, emotional, social and physical development through highly accessible programming options."

The Children's Room is resilient. Over the course of its life, the number and capacity of its board and volunteers have fluctuated. Being mostly made up of parents with young children, the turnover rate is high, as children inevitably age out of the programs within a few years. However, its rent-free location and the low overhead costs afforded by its volunteer-led structure have enabled it to adjust programs and scale up or down accordingly. The room benefited tremendously under the steady and skilled direction of Anne Latulippe, a resident of Duxbury. Naomi Alfini, a room user and board member, was hired to replace Anne upon her retirement in 2018. The location of the room has also moved around to accommodate the school's changing space needs—at least five times since 2000. During the 2006–07 school year, it was temporarily relocated to the Seminary Arts building in Waterbury Center while Thatcher Brook underwent renovations. The room is currently housed in the school's basement.

In the spring of 2017, the Children's Room was notified that, due to the ever-growing space needs of the school, its lease with Thatcher Brook would not be renewed for the following school year. Community members, particularly room users, reacted with shock and upset. The community voiced their concerns during a forum, and the school and district administration changed course and notified the Children's Room that the lease would be renewed for another year. Since then, the Children's Room lease with the school has in fact been renewed twice more, including the 2020–21 school year.

However, the arrival of the present COVID-19 pandemic has meant that in actuality, the Children's Room has not been able to hold any programs in the school since March 2020. While materials continue to be stored there, the board offered the room as a space for the school to use during this time while restriction measures require children and teachers to find ways to spread out and meet in smaller groups. As Vermonters were directed by Governor Scott to stay at home for all but essential tasks, the Children's Room quickly pivoted to offer online resources to support families. The families of the coordinator, Naomi, and board members Erin Hurley (co-chair) and Angeline Coyne livestreamed weekly Storytime and Music & Movement "playgroups" from their homes on Facebook, responding to the comments and questions sent in by live viewers during each session. Local children's musicians Andrea Soberman of Musical Munchkins and Rachel O'Donald of AB2 Braindance also contributed livestream concerts on the room's Facebook page. In another effort to reach vulnerable parents isolated at home, the Children's Room partnered with Good Beginnings of Central Vermont and the Women's Health Department of Central Vermont Medical Center to host a virtual support group (Baby Circle) for new and expecting parents, which meets weekly over Zoom. The Room also began organizing outdoor gatherings in response to families' needs and changing guidance for safety protocols. The room is hosting small

Singalong music activity for preschoolers in the Children's Room located at the Brookside Primary School. *Courtesy of the Children's Room.*

group playdates outdoors as weather allows, such as stroller strolls for caregivers with infants who can be contained in carriers and strollers and nature walks for toddlers and young children with their adults.

In the summer of 2020, the Children's Room also expanded its focus to supporting families and early educators in the community to do the work with young children required to heal the divides of racism. In June, as communities nationwide began reckoning with racism after the killing of George Floyd in Minneapolis, local families began speaking publicly about racism students were experiencing in the HUUSD district. In response, the Children's Room collaborated with longtime local partner in rights advocacy Maroni Minter of the ACLU (previously of Let's Grow Kids) to bring together families, school staff and wider community members in a rally attended by an estimated five hundred participants, to begin to recognize and understand the issues, express solidarity with area residents of color and affirm the value of the lives of Black people. Subsequently, they organized an in-person workshop on how to talk to young children about race, racism and anti-racism, with the Full Story School at Camp Meade.

The Children's Room's plans to continue working for families with young children in these ways, virtually and in small groups outdoors as a hub of information and social and emotional support until the pandemic lifts. The hope is to keep adapting programs to meet the evolving needs of families with young children, with the constant goal of providing a space and means for them to become better connected with the community; access opportunities to share positive experiences; and develop richer social networks and relationships, knowledge and tools to live happy, healthy lives.

3

CHILDREN'S LITERACY FOUNDATION (CLiF)

Duncan McDougall

Mission

The Children's Literacy Foundation (CLiF) is a nonprofit with a mission to nurture a love of reading and writing among low-income, at-risk and rural children from birth to age twelve throughout New Hampshire and Vermont.

History

CLiF was founded in 1998 by Duncan McDougall. He had been a writer and teacher and had tutored refugees. He also spent seven years working as a management consultant in Boston. Duncan loved working with children and had witnessed firsthand the transformative impact literacy skills had on children's likelihood of success in school, work and life. He decided to quit his consulting job and began planning CLiF.

Impact

Over twenty-three years, CLiF has served 300,000 children in more than 420 towns across New Hampshire and Vermont. All our services are completely free. Through our nine programs—and with the partnership of more than

Duncan McDougall, director of the Children's Literary Fund (CLiF), shares a delightful children's book with children. *Courtesy of CLiF.*

sixty-five professional authors, illustrators, poets, storytellers and graphic novelists—CLiF helps low-income, at-risk and rural children to love books, stories and words.

CLiF provides free, inspiring literacy programs and new books to children of prison inmates; refugee, migrant and foster children; children who live in shelters and low-income housing; and children served by bookmobiles, Head Start, Boys and Girls Clubs and other social service organizations. CLiF sponsors rural libraries, elementary schools and prisons and provides programs to dozens of other sites that serve children.

Many of the children in CLiF's target audience have few or no books of their own. Providing these kids access to inspiring new books is a key part of CLiF's mission. As of 2020, CLiF has donated $8 million in new, high-quality children's books to those children who need them the most.

Any way you measure it, CLiF has made an amazing amount of progress since we began:

- In 1998, attendance at our events was five hundred. In 2020, it was almost fifty thousand.
- In our first year, we gave away $7,400 in books. This year, we donated more than $875,000 in new, high-quality books to

children, many of whom have few or no books of their own at home. Each child gets to select whatever books they wish from hundreds of titles.

- We started by serving six communities in our first year. We now serve more than 175 different towns each year in every corner of New Hampshire and Vermont.
- For the first couple of years, Duncan was CLiF's only staff member and presenter. Today, the CLiF team is composed of more than one hundred energetic and motivated individuals, including five staff members, sixty-five professional presenters, ten directors, twelve advisors and fifteen-plus volunteers.
- We started with a single program (Rural Library Sponsorships) that involved a one-day visit to each sponsored town. We now run nine programs, most of which involve multifaceted and highly coordinated multiyear partnerships with the communities and organizations we serve.

Funding

Unlike most nonprofits, CLiF is supported entirely by individuals, foundations, companies and social organizations. It has more than seven hundred donors from thirty-five states and three countries.

Future

CLiF is very proud to be based in Waterbury, and we hope to stay here for many years to come. During this time of COVID-19, when schools and libraries are closed or working remotely and when many children's programs are not operating, CLiF's support of low-income, at-risk and rural children is more important than ever. In 2023, we will celebrate twenty-five years of working in Waterbury. We are striving to create an organization that will last one hundred years and continue inspiring millions of young readers and writers who need our help the most.

4

CENTRAL VERMONT ADULT BASIC EDUCATION IN WATERBURY

Brian Kravitz

Central Vermont Adult Basic Education Inc. (CVABE) has been proudly serving Waterbury since 1965. Our overarching goal is to provide career and college readiness education that leads to financial independence and long-term generational success. Our core programs are functional literacy, high school credentialing and English Language Learning/Civics. We serve nearly five hundred central Vermont residents annually, forty to fifty through our Waterbury Learning Center.

Beginning in the 1970s, our instructors traveled throughout their service areas, doing direct outreach and providing in-home literacy instruction. By the early-1980s, the uniqueness of the Waterbury area shone through. With the State Hospital in town, as well as a high need for adult education services, CVABE rose to the challenge and added Waterbury as its third learning center location (preceded by Barre and Morrisville).

In the early 2000s, to further strengthen and promote its program identity, CVABE added the tagline "local partnerships in learning." This represented the central shared belief that CVABE's literacy mission can be achieved only by way of real, practical partnership with the many and varied communities of central Vermont. The tagline is a reminder, in fact, of CVABE's dual mission: providing basic education instruction for adults and teens and involving the entire community in the encouragement of their efforts.

Community volunteers are our closest partners in learning. The Waterbury community has provided CVABE with over twenty-five volunteers at any given time. They offer their expertise to our students and also create valuable connections between those students and the larger community. These partnerships run deep in Waterbury.

Hurricane Irene, in 2011, had a devastating effect on Waterbury, yet at the same time it brought the community closer together. Through the pain and heartache, we saw the amazing community that Waterbury was, and the ground was set for the next decade. In the years since Irene, Waterbury has grown and changed and has truly found its role as "Vermont's recreation crossroads." CVABE continues in Waterbury, always adapting to the changing needs of the town and excited to be an integral part of the community's growth.

We serve adults and teens without high school credentials, those with low literacy and those with low English skills. We also provide educational services to adults who have high school credentials and sometimes even some college but who have reading, writing, math or computer skills less than a high school equivalent. As the needs of the local population and businesses grow and change, we will be right there, helping the community to reach its goals.

CVABE has consistently served the Waterbury community for fifty-five years, and we have helped thousands of residents read, write, do math, operate computers, learn English, prepare for citizenship, gain high school credentials and attain the skills to transition to career and college. We look forward to serving Waterbury for the next fifty-five years, helping both residents and businesses meet their needs and reach their goals. We are honored to be a local partner in learning in Waterbury's vibrant community.

PART VIII

ENERGY, RECYCLING AND RENEWABLES

1

GREEN UP DAY

Adapted from the Town of Waterbury Annual Report for the Year Ending December 31, 2020.

Green Up Vermont is a nonprofit private organization that relies on the Town of Waterbury's support each year to execute the tradition of cleaning up our roadways and waterways, while promoting civic pride. The tradition of Green Up Day began in 1970 by Governor Deane Davis and celebrated its fiftieth year in May 2020. Many individuals and families look forward to signing up for a location to "green up" each year.

Local community children proudly participate in the annual Green Up Day event. *Courtesy of Gordon Miller.*

2

THE MAD RIVER RESOURCE ALLIANCE

John Malter

The Mad River Resource Management Alliance (MRRMA) provides management of municipal solid waste through an interlocal agreement between the towns of Waterbury, Fayston, Moretown, Waitsfield and Warren. The purpose of the interlocal agreement is to ensure the efficient implementation of the Solid Waste Implementation Plan (SWIP). While all of this might sound a bit bureaucratic and acronym laden, it's just the vehicle that our town's residents and businesses use to reduce their waste lines.

Since the year 2000, there have been several significant events in the world of solid waste here in the MRRMA. In 2000, the Mad River Solid Waste Alliance was one of three pilot sites for the collection of electronic waste, referred to as e-waste. (This became a law in Vermont in 2011.) In 2008, the name of the Alliance was changed from the Mad River Solid Waste Alliance to the MRRMA. This was done to reflect the fact that we are managing resources, not wastes.

Another event was Tropical Storm Irene in 2011, which resulted in the need to collect and recycle over 49.50 tons of tires and over 12.58 tons of household hazardous waste during the cleanup of residences, businesses and riverbanks in the MRRMA.

A third event was the closure of the Moretown Landfill in 2013, when the capacity of cell three of the landfill was reached and the certification expired. This resulted in the loss of the facility, which provided on-site solid waste disposal and a variety of recycling programs, including single stream, book, records, CDs, electronic waste, used crankcase oil, oil filters, textiles recycling and budgetary support.

The fourth major event occurred when Ed Steele, who had been Waterbury's representative to the MRRMA since its inception and figured prominently in its development, retired from the board in 2014. Alec Tuscany has been the Waterbury representative to the board since 2014.

The major programs that the MRRMA accomplishes include the Household Hazardous Waste Collections held twice a year in the spring and fall—they collect over 14.00 tons of material annually. Through both the program at Grow Compost and the use of backyard composting bins, we average the diversion of approximately 567.00 tons of food scraps that create rich compost for garden use. During Green Up Day, the first Saturday in May except when there is a pandemic, the MRRMA has averaged over 14.49 tons of tires that have been collected from various cleanup activities. Our e-waste collections have averaged over 36.10 tons annually. One of the sites to bring e-waste to is the State Surplus Property facility on Route 2 in Waterbury. You can find out more about our programs at our website: madriverrma.org.

3

SUNCOMMON

Duanne Peterson

SunCommon employs 120 Vermonters with good pay, great benefits and a fulfilling mission. But the story of how the Waterbury company became the largest provider of solar power in Vermont begins, ironically, with a climate crisis: Hurricane Irene.

SunCommon cofounders Duane Peterson and James Moore met at Vermont Public Interest Research Group (VPIRG), the state's leading environmental advocacy organization. Deeply concerned about the unfolding climate crisis, they sought to understand why the country's response had been so inadequate. A transition to clean energy, away from burning fossil fuels in the open atmosphere, was the obvious answer. Yet adoption of clean, safe, local and cheaper renewables was painfully slow. Duane and James saw the urgent need for a consumer solution, so they built a new enterprise that focused on making solar power easy and affordable to homeowners and businesses.

The pilot effort showed that folks clearly wanted solar but needed someone to do the legwork. That's where SunCommon stepped in. But to meet growing demand, the newly minted solar entrepreneurs needed to scale up their enterprise. Their small solar project quickly outgrew its VPIRG home, and outside capital was raised to allow the venture to meet its mission. SunCommon became an independent venture and one of Vermont's first Benefit Corporations committed to the triple bottom line of people, planet and profit.

The company's novel 2011 business plan included raising the money needed to launch, advancing an innovative go-to-market strategy, hiring eighteen employees to start, leasing a fleet of high-mileage hybrid cars, partnering with other likeminded socially responsible businesses and selling the highest-quality solar equipment available. The next step was deciding where to put this promising start-up.

James and his wife lived in Montpelier, and Duane and his family lived in Essex. Sensing that those population centers would provide both employees and customers, they wanted to locate somewhere in between. Looking up and down Interstate 89, Waterbury jumped off the map as just having suffered the ravages of Tropical Storm Irene. "Irene Lays Waste to Waterbury Village" blared the headline. So, Duane and James committed to setting up shop there and contributing what they could to the reinvigoration of the town.

They knew SunCommon would not revive Waterbury single-handedly, but just as ripples spread out when a single pebble is dropped into water, the actions of individuals can have far-reaching effects. Duane and James hoped the new venture could add a little boost to the rebuilding of the hurting community.

Whatever SunCommon's cofounders knew about starting a new solar business, they knew less about commercial real estate. But a key to their success had always been seeking out folks who knew what they did not, and they had assembled a wide network of experts over their decades of work in Vermont. As it turned out, ReBuild Waterbury was headed by Jeanne Kirby, whose husband had run VPIRG. Jeanne introduced Duane to Waterbury realtor Cindy Lyons who, after hearing about the planned solar venture, said simply, "Get in the car," and drove up Waterbury-Stowe Road to a field with a sign that touted the Energy Mill—A Place for Sustainable Businesses. Beyond the sign, there was a concrete pad with steel girders going up and a crew of workers. Gristmill Builders' Brendan O'Reilly, who had envisioned the complex and was supervising the build, described the project as Vermont's largest energy-positive building (meaning it would generate more power than it used), made from local materials, built by local craftspeople and intended as home for businesses looking to do right. Duane, James and Brendan shook on the deal for SunCommon to be the anchor tenant, and the solar business set up shop on February 1, 2012.

The Energy Mill was wonderful digs for the start-up SunCommon. Its physical environment conveyed the company's local and sustainable values. And Waterbury welcomed SunCommon as another thriving business—with employees shopping for lunch, gas, books and groceries in SunCommon's cheerfully decorated vehicles. Waterbury was home.

SunCommon's success saw its workforce grow from the eighteen who first occupied the Energy Mill to fifty, busting at the seams. A lot more space was needed, and even more would be needed in the coming years, so the company needed to move on from the Energy Mill after three great years.

There was no question that SunCommon wanted to stay in Waterbury, the community that so welcomed the new solar business. But again, where to locate? Duane and James went to Revitalizing Waterbury and the economic development advisors who knew the town's landscape and the possibilities. If new construction were an option, the land hosting the Waterbury Flea Market was for sale. No way was SunCommon going to boot the beloved Flea Market. Luckily, the market was moving anyway, to a preferable space farther down Route 2.

The people at SunCommon knew little about commercial real estate and really needed to focus on their own business—so how could they get their headquarters built? Once again, the experts at Revitalizing Waterbury introduced SunCommon to the right people.

Of all the proposed developers, Pat Malone stood out. He drove his Subaru to the meeting, wearing Carhartts and flannel. During due diligence, Pat was asked how many such buildings he had built in Vermont. He was not sure. Like a dozen, or a few dozen? Maybe a hundred, he said. He was the real deal.

SunCommon wanted its flagship facility to be energy positive and made from local materials by local craftspeople. Employees wanted an open, airy interior—and, of course, as a start-up they were cost conscious. The company turned to Waitsfield architect Bill Maclay, a prominent member of Vermont Businesses for Social Responsibility and literally the author of the book (*NetZero Architecture*). He and his firm designed the building as Vermont's largest energy-positive structure to showcase SunCommon's clean energy offerings.

But the deal was for Malone Properties to build the facility, own it and lease it back to SunCommon. Malone did not want to build a Taj Mahal (lest SunCommon fail and he be left with a tricked-out building he could not re-rent), and SunCommon needed to invest its cash in growing the business, rather than in lavish digs. So Maclay designed a simple but gorgeous building whose energy efficiency and clean power generation indeed cost more to build than mere code required. But with no fuel costs to heat, cool or power the building (sunshine is free), the monthly costs to inhabit and operate the building were expected to be on par with standard construction. This was a novel notion, but Malone jumped in. A joyful moment was when the crew from Malone Properties saw the results of the building envelope efficiency test—they beamed with pride at the quality of the work they had done. In the entryway to the building is a plaque naming each of the one hundred local craftspeople who created the SunCommon headquarters: steelworkers, concrete pourers, fabricators, drywall hangers, painters, designers, artists and engineers. It's a testament to the community.

SunCommon moved in May 2016. The new building had space to hold events, especially the monthly all-company meetings that gather the entire workforce for open-book financials, news of the business and personal reflections. Public officials often visit the SunCommon workforce, and community groups use the space for their meetings. To celebrate its connection to the Waterbury community, SunCommon throws an annual Summer Solstice Celebration for four hundred of its employees, customers, business partners and community collaborators. There is always plenty of food, music and cheer. Every year has brought spectacular weather, owing to the business's special relationship with the sun.

The beginning of 2020 saw 140 SunCommon employees working out of Waterbury and another 40 in New York's Hudson Valley, where SunCommon acquired a leading solar business. The year of the pandemic seriously disrupted SunCommon when state mandates shuttered the business for two months. But with welcome support from federal disaster relief, the business reconfigured to operate safely and reopened with the same resolve to address the climate crisis and use the power of business for good. It's back to growing—to provide more job opportunities, build more clean energy and serve its nine thousand solar customers across two states, all from its home in Waterbury, Vermont.

4

WATERBURY LEAP

Duncan McDougall

In early 2007, Duncan McDougall recruited several local Waterbury residents, and together they organized the first annual Waterbury Renewable Energy and Energy Efficiency Rally as part of the nationwide Step-It-Up Day on April 14. The event was a standing-room-only success. The attendees overflowed the Waterbury Senior Center and then formed a noisy, colorful parade that streamed down Waterbury's Main Street.

On that day, almost fifty people signed up, indicating that they were interested in continuing local efforts to reduce carbon emissions and promote energy efficiency and the use of renewable resources in Waterbury and the surrounding area. Waterbury LEAP (Local Energy Action Partnership) was born.

LEAP's mission is to promote energy efficiency and the use of renewable energy and to engage our community in reducing carbon emissions in Waterbury, Vermont, and the surrounding area.

From the very beginning, LEAP has been an independent organization fueled by the energy and ideas of local volunteer members. We support our town leaders whenever possible, but we are not officially affiliated with the Town of Waterbury. We have about fifteen members who are actively involved in our projects and another forty who help when needed. Current board members include Trevor Luce, Duncan McDougall, Rich Rivers, Steve Sisler, Brian Wagner, Kit Walker and Brian Woods.

LEAP is one of more than 115 Vermont town energy committees and is recognized as one of the most active and productive such organizations in the state. In recent years, LEAP has received various statewide energy awards for its work, including the Governor's Award for Environmental Excellence and energy leadership awards from Vermont Natural Resources Council (VNRC), the Vermont Energy & Climate Action Network (VECAN) and Renewable Energy Vermont (REV).

LEAP is the only town energy committee in Vermont to become a 501(c)(3) nonprofit. We took that step because we wanted to provide as much support as possible to our neighbors as they consider their green energy options. Since our founding in April 2007, LEAP's many volunteers have completed dozens of exciting local projects. Among many other activities, LEAP has:

- Hosted an annual LEAP Energy Fair, the largest energy fair in Vermont. The event outgrew two other venues, and it now draws seventy-five-plus green energy exhibitors and more than seven hundred attendees at this free community gathering held at Crossett Brook Middle School
- Hosted annual Button Up Weatherization and Home Heating seminars in the late fall to help local residents tighten up their homes
- Hosted Electric Vehicle Fests that typically include fifteen to twenty different electric vehicles, 150 attendees, local EV owners and an expert from Drive Electric Vermont
- Hosted Solar and Heat Pump Fests in the summer that bring together solar and heat pump experts with those who want to learn about how to save money and energy by using those technologies
- Helped place solar arrays on Thatcher Brook Primary School and Crossett Brook Middle School. For several years, CBMS, with 172 kilowatts in solar arrays, had the greatest solar capacity of any school in Vermont
- Helped replace local streetlights with LED bulbs and distributed thousands of compact fluorescent bulbs and hundreds of LED bulbs
- Started Waterbury in Motion, a program to help develop and expand a bike/pedestrian system in town. We hold a Bike & Walk to School Day every spring and fall that draws 200 to 250 attendees at each event
- Developed strong ties with students and teachers at Crossett Brook Middle School and Harwood Union High School to support them

Bike or walk to school event, one of many activities promoted by the Local Energy Action Partnership (LEAP). *Courtesy of Duncan McDougall.*

in pursuing green energy projects. Every year at the LEAP Energy Fair we give the Waterbury LEAP Green Community Award to "the student or team of students with the best project related to energy efficiency, renewable energy, or emissions reduction."
- Assisted town leaders in writing the Waterbury Energy Plan, which has fifty-two action items. LEAP members are on the committee currently charged with helping enact those action items.

LEAP volunteers feel strongly it is in our society's, and our environment's, best interest if humans reduce their emissions and increase their adoption of energy efficiency and renewable energy efforts quickly and substantially. We are concerned with the slow pace adopted by leaders in the United States and around the world.

We also believe that most people want to save money and energy, and so we provide them access to the experts, information and the support they need to move forward on their projects.

Climate change is an existential threat to us and our planet. Our hope for Waterbury is that our community continues to be a green energy leader and innovator, helping protect the local environment that we love and cherish; keeping our dollars local; and assisting our residents, businesses and the municipality to experience a significant reduction in fuel usage and expenses. "If the people lead, the leaders will follow."

PART IX

MUNICIPAL GOVERNMENT

1

THE FORTUNES OF THE WATERBURY MUNICIPAL OFFICE AND TWO HISTORIC BUILDINGS

Skip Flanders

The first twenty years of the twenty-first century in Waterbury resulted in very different outcomes for two historic buildings involving the municipal office. The Waterbury Town and Village Office was originally located in a historic house at 51 South Main Street. This building and lot have connections dating back to Waterbury's first settler, James Marsh. The early history reports that James Marsh's oldest son Elias owned the property in the 1790s and built a house on Lot 5 in the second division of the 1763 plotting plan. Elias died on March 29, 1802, and is buried in an unmarked grave in Hope Cemetery.

The next owner, Cephas Wells, who settled in Waterbury in 1805 from Greenfield, Massachusetts, was a tanner and farmer and constructed the current house in the 1815 to 1825 period. This house is similar to the Dan Carpenter House across the street at 60 South Main Street, constructed in 1816. Cephas Wells died in 1849, and relatives lived in the house until 1869. The property was then purchased by Thaddeus B. Crossett, and his wife, Roxanna, lived in the house for sixty-five years, until she died in 1934.

Charles Parker purchased the house from the Crossett estate in 1934 and made many improvements. After Charlie Parker and his wife passed away, his son Craig "Rusty" Parker owned the house. Rusty, as he was known because of his red hair, was a longtime member of the Select Board and a radio announcer on WDEV. Rusty suffered a heart attack while on the air and died in 1982.

In 1983, the Village of Waterbury voted to purchase the property for use as the Town and Village Municipal Office. Renovations were made, including a fireproof records vault and a police station in the barn. The municipal offices continued in the building until Hurricane Irene occurred on August 28, 2011. The building suffered flood damage and oil contamination caused by the oil tank in the basement tipping over and spilling oil, soaking the floor joists, carpet and flooring. This contamination needed to be remediated before repairs could be made. During that time the municipal offices were located in the elementary school and the police station in the recreation building near the swimming pool.

Soon after the flood, the Select Board determined that the building at 51 South Main Street was not sufficient to meet the growing needs of the community, and it was necessary to explore options for expanded facilities. DEW Construction provided the village trustees an estimate that it would cost $435,000 to restore the old municipal office to its preexisting condition. Considering the shortcomings of the building and the decision of the Select Board not to return, the trustees decided to take a reduced amount of $350,000 of insurance money and explore other uses of the property rather than restore the building. It was eventually decided to take the building down. The trustees wanted to salvage as much material as possible and hired Deconstruction Works for the deconstruction. The building removal was completed in 2019, the lot paved and used for off street parking while Main Street was reconstructed in 2019–21.

With the municipal office severely damaged and the building not adequate for future needs, the Select Board, library commissioners and village trustees formed the Municipal Building Committee to search for new options to meet the community's needs. This search was incorporated as a key part of the Irene Long Term Recovery Plan. State officials agreed to sell the town a two-acre property at the end of Randall Street that included Stanley and Wasson Hall for $300,000. Black River Architects was hired to prepare a design that included municipal offices, a library and space for the village police department. This proposal, with an estimated total cost of $7.75 million, was supported by $1.25 million in recovery grants, funding from the village and library commissioners but a $5 million town bond was voted down 570 to 742 on June 13, 2013.

The Municipal Building Committee then considered the site of the existing library located in the historic Dr. Janes House on North Main Street adjacent to Dac Rowe Field. This property was settled by Dr. Janes's father, Henry Janes, in 1817. Dr. Janes, a Civil War surgeon and local doctor, built

Renovation of the Henry Janes building, located at 48 South Main Street in Waterbury. *Courtesy of Gordon Miller.*

the Queen Anne–style cottage in 1881 and bequeathed the property upon his death in 1915 to the town to be used as a library. Vermont Integrated Architecture was hired to develop a proposal for a building including municipal office, library and space for the historical society. Space for the police department was not included in this proposal. The design included rehabilitating the Dr. Janes House to include offices and museum space for the historical society. The estimated total cost of the project was $5 million. The total funding included a $2.95 million municipal bond, $1.25 million in recovery grants and $1 million in private funding. On March 14, 2014, a bond vote for $2.95 million was passed, 809 to 617. A petition was submitted to rescind the bond vote, and a vote to rescind was defeated on May 13, 2014, 493 to 917.

The final design was completed, and the low bid of $4.98 million was submitted by ReArch. Construction was started on April 13, 2015, and an open house held on February 12, 2016. The building, with its energy-efficient design, is the pride of Waterbury and has served the community well and will for future decades to come.

The future of two of Waterbury's historic buildings that had served the community for decades had very different outcomes in the first two decades of the twenty-first century. The property at 51 South Main Street served as the municipal office for twenty-seven years, suffered severe damage and was taken down—the future use of the property is to be determined. The historic Dr. Janes residence that housed a municipal library for one hundred years is rehabilitated and incorporated as a part of a new complex to serve the community into the twenty-second century. Such is the fate at the hands of Mother Nature. The early founders and settlers of Waterbury are to be commended for their construction; their buildings have given decades of commendable service to those who followed them. It is hoped that the decisions made by Waterbury residents in the first two decades of the twenty-first century can serve the future as well as those of the founding fathers.

2

PLANNING

Cindy Parks, adapted from an interview with Steve Lotspeich

The following information is based on an interview conducted by Cindy Parks with Steve Lotspeich, the full-time professional planner overseeing the planning department. He has worked as Waterbury's planner for twenty-eight years, and in 2017, he received the Professional Planner of the Year Award from the Vermont Planners Association. As a planner, Steve is considered a Renaissance man and must be knowledgeable in a breadth of subjects, including natural resources, transportation, utilities, municipal facilities and services, energy, housing, cultural/historic/scenic resources, land use and flood resilience/hazard mitigation. The planning department also includes Dina Bookmyer-Baker, who has been the full-time zoning administrator since 2016.

The planning department is responsible for writing and implementing the Municipal Plan, most recently updated in 2018. This plan was developed through working with local citizens and community leaders to provide a collaborative vision for how Waterbury should grow, both in the short and long term, through a balance of development, environmental conservation and historic preservation. Planning and the related zoning program include the work of the planning commission, development review board, conservation commission and tree committee.

The first two decades of the twenty-first century have seen many important and major planning and construction projects in Waterbury. Several of these projects have evolved from the impact of and recovery from Tropical Storm Irene.

Planning Projects

Zoning: Establishment of the Ridgelines, Hillsides and Steep Slopes Overlay District. During the 2003 update of the Municipal Plan, there was discussion regarding whether to prohibit development in areas of Waterbury above 1,500 feet in elevation due to the sensitive and scenic environment. The establishment of the Ridgelines, Hillsides, Steep Slopes Overlay District seeks to regulate, rather than prohibit, development above 1,200 feet. The planning commission and staff led this initiative. The genesis was a 2004 to 2005 study analyzing steep slope areas in Waterbury by the consultant Landworks of Middlebury, with UVM wildlife biology professor David Capen serving as a subconsultant. The study resulted in the creation of additional zoning regulations, including the overlay district for development at elevations over 1,200 feet.

Establishment of Designated Downtown. This initiative was done in conjunction with Waterbury's downtown organization, Revitalizing Waterbury Inc. Design review bylaws had to be developed to allow regulatory control and a Downtown Design Review Overlay District created, which matched the boundaries of the Designated Downtown area. Part of Pilgrim Industrial Park is included in the Overlay District. The Downtown Development Board of the VT Agency of Commerce and Community Development approved Waterbury's Designated Downtown in 2006. Waterbury's downtown program is organized and led by Revitalizing Waterbury. The program includes marketing, promotion and beautification for the Designated Downtown.

A parallel Designated Village Center was created in Waterbury Center Village in 2016. Both the Designated Downtown and Village Center include the promotion of historic resources. Tax credits are available to support improvements to historic buildings.

Resurvey of the Waterbury Village Historic District and Individual Listed Properties. The Waterbury Village Historic District is one of six historic districts in Waterbury. All six districts and over thirty individually listed historic properties were originally surveyed in 1976. All the historic resources in the survey are included in the VT State Register of Historic Places. Some are also listed in the National Register of Historic Places due to significant architectural and building trades values, recreational and transportation history and events/people important to VT's history. The Village Historic District composes a larger area than the Designated Downtown. In 2018, the Waterbury Village Historic District was resurveyed by Scott Newman of 106 Associates. This resulted in an expansion of the district to include all eligible structures and additional areas of historic buildings.

Creation of the Green Mountain Byway. This seventy-one-mile corridor that surrounds Routes 100 and 15 travels through Waterbury, Stowe, Morristown, Hyde Park, Johnson and Cambridge. It is part of the National Byway Program, whose mission is to recognize, preserve and enhance selected scenic roads throughout the country. The byway is governed by a steering committee, which is composed of representatives from two regional planning commissions, the six towns and the associated villages, historical societies, the Vermont Department of Forests, Parks and Recreation and at-large members. The steering committee undertakes and supports projects that balance the promotion, preservation, enjoyment and stewardship of the byway's intrinsic values. A Corridor Management Plan for Route 100 was prepared in 2004 by the consultant Landworks of Middlebury, Vermont.

Associated Recreation and Cultural/Historic Guides were created for Stowe and Waterbury as part of the byway project. Grant funding was obtained to install eighteen interpretive panels associated with the byway.

Construction Projects

Green Mountain Seminary Building. This structure is located on Hollow Road in Waterbury Center. In the early and mid-twentieth century, it was the location of the Waterbury Graded School, until on-site wastewater issues led to its condemnation for a school. This underutilized structure was owned by Eric and Francine Chittenden until 2000, when it was developed into sixteen apartments, primarily for people of low to medium income. The project was completed in 2001 by the Central Vermont Community Land Trust, now known as Downstreet Housing & Community Development. The Town of Waterbury helped facilitate the project by applying for a community block grant, providing a loan from the town's revolving loan fund and making adjacent land available by reorienting the existing baseball field. The soil has high percolating rates for an on-site wastewater system. In 2007, the Waterbury Center Library, also housed in the Seminary Building, was closed and reconverted into a pottery studio and gallery for Mame McKee's Seminary Arts program. Today, Makerspace owns and operates the studio.

Reconstruction of the Waterbury Train Station. Businessman Jack Carter and planner Steve Lotspeich, in looking together at an enlarged postcard of the station circa 1900, both dreamed of redeveloping the station. This building was originally constructed in 1848 but was destroyed and reconstructed in 1875.

The Village of Waterbury secured a Vermont Agency of Transportation Enhancement Grant for a feasibility study in the late 1990s. The two major components of the study were to (1) develop schematic architectural plans and prepare a cost estimate for reconstructing the original building; and (2) conduct the associated public process to establish possible future uses for the building.

Following a series of public meetings to determine how to use the building, the final selected alternative was to construct a café and visitor's center and to continue the Amtrak services. Independently, Green Mountain Coffee Roasters (GMCR) was interested in developing a visitor's center for the business. Paul Comey from GMCR worked with the project steering committee to study the restoration of the building. It had been decided during the feasibility study to conduct the construction in two phases due to the estimated costs in excess of $1 million. The Stiller Foundation decided to get behind the project financially by providing funding in excess of $400,000. A second enhancement grant in the amount of $365,000 allowed the full reconstruction project to become viable.

Arnold & Scangas Architects from St. Albans was selected for the final design of the restoration. The lead architect, Laz Scangas, is a railroad buff and helped implement the vision to connect the main railway station and the baggage building using glass. The building restoration was completed in 2006. Scangas donated the two mileage signs posted on the narrow ends of the building. Revitalizing Waterbury Inc. eventually was able to purchase the building from the New England Central Railway.

Tropical Storm Irene Recovery and Reconstruction of the State Office Complex. Nineteen projects were identified during the long-term community recovery initiative. Several involved extensive input from the planning department through revamping of the flood hazard regulations, rewriting the zoning regulations and the implementation of a flood plain management program.

Additional major recovery projects associated with Tropical Storm Irene in Waterbury were

- new municipal offices and public library complex
- conversion of Ladd Hall into the Main Street Apartments

- reconstruction of the Whalley Mobile Home Park; and
- rehabilitation and reconstruction of the state office complex.

The only outstanding recovery projects currently are the forthcoming demolition of Stanley and Wasson Halls on the campus of the former Vermont State Hospital.

ROUNDABOUT PROJECT. The planning department did a transportation, parking and circulation study in 1999 prepared by the consultant Peter Hart, AICP, with Community Planning & Design. The study included evaluating the intersection of North Main Street and Route 100. The major alternatives considered were designing and constructing a roundabout or using eighteen signals to control traffic flow and enhance public safety. As part of the study, subconsultant Buckhurst Fish & Jacquemart (BFJ Planning) from New York City prepared the conceptual design of the roundabout using a plan developed by volunteer engineering consultant Doug Weber from Duxbury. The village trustees chose the alternative of the roundabout. The consulting firm, Stantec, prepared the final design of the roundabout, including access and reconstructed parking areas for the post office and Maxi's Restaurant.

3
PUBLIC WORKS DEPARTMENT

Cindy Parks

The following information was gathered by Cindy Parks through an interview with current Waterbury Public Works director Bill Woodruff, former Waterbury Public Works director and current town and village engineer Alec Tuscany and chief operator of the Edward Farrar Utility District (EFUD) of the Wastewater Treatment Plant Peter Krolczyk.

The past two decades have been very busy for the public works department with extensive activities—both planned maintenance and upgrades as well as unplanned, primarily in response to climate events. This includes updates to the wastewater system, installation of renewable energy systems and projects that resulted from the impact of Tropical Storm Irene.

Wastewater System

Waterbury's Wastewater System and staff have received national accolades under the leadership of Alec Tuscany, Bill Woodruff and Peter Krolczyk with support from Bill Shepeluk, town manager, and the water and sewer commissioners. This includes the Energy Efficiency Award for Solar-Powered Mixers in Outdoor Aeration Ponds. Using a grant provided by Efficiency VT, the seven ten-horsepower electric mixing motors in the aeration ponds were replaced with three solar-powered Grid Bee© lagoon circulators. The circulators provide oxygen to the micro-organisms consuming the waste material. Annual cost savings of 40 percent were achieved, and the sludge production was reduced by using the Grid Bee© circulators. These positive outcomes were documented in the July 2018 issue of *Treatment Plant Operator*, a national publication for wastewater professionals.

Waterbury's Wastewater Treatment Plant also received the National EPA PISCES Award for using phosphorus removal technology. In 2005, the State of Vermont ordered all wastewater treatment plants (WWTPs) discharging to the Lake Champlain Basin to install phosphorus removal to protect and improve the lake's water quality. Waterbury embarked on a $7.6 million, ten-year project, which can remove up to 98 percent of the phosphorus in the wastewater. The plant is the first one in Vermont to use ballasted flocculation phosphorus removal, installed downstream of the existing three-cell aerated lagoon WWTP. This award is a distinct honor given its national scope.

In 2018, Peter Krolczyk, chief operator of the Edward Farrar Utility District (EFUD) WWTP, was the recipient of the Operator Excellence Award in Wastewater from the Green Mountain Water Environment Association. Peter has thirty years of experience and holds the highest grade of operator certification available. In addition, he volunteers his time operating and maintaining both the drinking water and wastewater systems for his faith organization.

Sewer Updates

The local sewer ordinance is entering a public comment period following long-needed update. The Utility District's sewer ordinance had not been updated since the Reagan administration. The revised ordinance is based on the most current technical standards and guidance. One of its major features is the ability to regulate high-strength wastes, including brewery, food preparation and distillery wastes at the local level.

Renewable Energy Systems

The town and Utility District have chosen a proactive approach to using renewable energy. The first municipal solar installation was constructed in 2011 on the roof of the rehabilitated Main Street Fire Station. Income is generated from leasing of these sites, and electricity revenue credits are applied to municipal or large users' (such as the Ice Center) electric bills.

The revenues from the Sweet Wellfield solar installation are credited to the WWTP's electrical costs and can pay up to one-third of the annual costs, which is significant, as wastewater treatment facilities are among the largest users of energy.

Impact of Tropical Storm Irene

Waterbury experienced significant infrastructure damage from Tropical Storm Irene in August 2011. The sewer mains on Elm and Main Streets ruptured. Scores of water service lines were broken but were shut off by the Water Department staff in a timely manner, preserving the public water storage volumes for firefighting and domestic use. Overall damage to interior plumbing in flooded buildings in Waterbury was estimated at $300,000 to $400,000.

Large sinkholes appeared in front of 51 South Main Street, the former location of the municipal offices, on Elm Street opposite the Municipal Parking Lot, with smaller sinkholes showing up at multiple other locations within the village. Cracks in the old sewer mains in front of 51 South Main Street and on Elm Street allowed floodwaters to enter, drawing the road subbase into the sewers, creating the sinkholes. The recently completed Main Street Project has reduced the chance of sinkholes reoccurring in the future.

Four town and village buildings were damaged, including the municipal offices at 51 South Main Street, the Main Street Fire Station, the Main Street Wastewater Pump Station and the town library. Upgrades to the Main Street Fire Station were completed prior to Irene. The facility was designed and constructed with concrete walls up to the one-hundred-year flood elevation and with all utilities located on the second floor, thereby minimizing the damage experienced. The interior of the Main Street Wastewater Pump Station was completely flooded, requiring replacement of pumps, motors, controls and generator. Gasketing on the flood doors had to be replaced to provide a watertight seal. The new generator is now situated outside on a concrete pad above the five-hundred-year flood level.

The storm also caused significant damage to the roadways near Winooski Street and River Road, the Dascomb P. Rowe and River Road Recreation fields, farmland adjacent to the WWTP used for drying sludge and surface water intake structures in the Worcester Range watershed, which filled with gravel and stone that required removal.

Future Challenges

The public works staff hold the opinion that climate change poses the greatest challenge now and moving forward. Both the frequency and magnitude of rainfall and snow events as well as the increase in droughts pose a challenge for all infrastructure systems. Vermont scientists are of the opinion that Tropical Storm Irene is now the new baseline for what was formerly known as the one-hundred-year storm. This new baseline is thirty inches higher than the previous historic one-hundred-year storm event. The location of Waterbury's downtown within the one-hundred-year floodplain, the flashiness of precipitation events in our mountainous areas combined with increasing development outside of town centers, the difficulty of predicting extreme weather events and the high capital cost of preparing for and mitigating weather events associated with climate change further add to the challenges.

4

WATERBURY TRANSPORTATION IMPROVEMENTS FROM 2000 TO 2021

Barb Farr

Waterbury has seen nearly a decade of steady transportation infrastructure construction improvements between 2012 and 2021 that have resulted in a long-awaited facelift and necessary infrastructure repairs. The town of Waterbury is known as the "Crossroads of Vermont," as it is conveniently located at the junction of I-89 and Routes 100/2 between Montpelier (the state capital), Burlington (the largest metropolitan area) and Stowe and Mad River Valley (high traffic recreational and tourist areas).

The Agency of Transportation and Town of Waterbury embarked on a several-decade-long initiative to identify necessary road enhancements and investments as early as the 1980s. This resulted in years of planning, design and engineering work, public meetings and hearings with the Town of Waterbury, and securing local, state and federal funds to accomplish the goals of making transportation improvements in Waterbury.

Waterbury has benefited in receiving approximately $60 million in improvements, with the vast majority coming from state and federal funding during this period of construction.

The roundabout project replaced an overloaded T intersection south of the I-89 interchange at the junction with Route 2. Following the completion of this project, traffic moves much more smoothly and efficiently around the roundabout. During the planning stages, the level of service at this intersection was classified as F, indicating frequent or long travel traffic delays.

In addition to replacing the T intersection with a roundabout, the project included new sidewalks to provide access to businesses, the post office and recreational facilities. The project, which was managed by the Town of Waterbury, included relocation/replacement of water, sanitary gravity sewer and sewer mains and construction of a new, safer entrance to the post office and restaurant with improved landscaping and parking.

I-89 Exit 10 Interchange, 2014–17, $11 Million—State and Federal

This project involved three major bridge replacements and the closure of one southbound lane entrance ramp. All southbound traffic has been directed to one entrance ramp. All federal and state funds were used in the I-89 and Exit 10 improvements as well as Stowe Street improvements and sidewalks under the bridges.

The I-89 Bridges Project rehabilitated aging components of the I-89 mainline substructure and replaced the concrete decks to extend the life of the northbound and southbound bridges and completely replaced the Exit 10 northbound off-ramp bridge.

The two mainline bridge decks had deteriorated to the point that concrete was starting to fall from the structure, triggering replacement. Work began in August 2014 and was completed in 2015. Work on the replacement bridge for the northbound off-ramp began in 2016. A new ramp bridge was built with two piers and three spans with continuous steel girders and expansion joints at the ends only.

The northbound exit ramp was widened to two lanes to provide additional capacity on the ramp because traffic occasionally backs up onto I-89 during special events and peak tourist season. Adaptive signal controls were also installed as part of the I-89 project. These signal controls include control boxes and cameras to track traffic at each segment of the interstate. This data enables VTrans to trace the history of traffic patterns and adjust signal phasing from the main VTrans traffic management center to accommodate better traffic flow.

Route 100 from I-89 to Stowe, 2016–18, $25 Million—State and Federal

This was a full-depth reconstruction of Route 100 that involved removing the concrete base roadway that was originally built in the 1930s as the first concrete road in Vermont. It was narrower than the current roadway standard and had to be repatched and repaved regularly due to the sides of the road continuously sinking and settling lower than the narrow concrete original roadway.

When this portion of roadway was completed in 2018, the transportation improvements between the two downtowns of Waterbury and Stowe had been significantly upgraded to include smooth travel surfaces, bike lanes (marked in some areas and widened in all areas) and a new traffic light at the intersection of Guptil Road and Route 100. This had been a frequent accident location, and it works much more efficiently following its installation.

Main Street Reconstruction, 2019–21, $22+ Million—State, Federal and Local

The Main Street reconstruction project was first included in the Vermont Agency of Transportation budget in 1982. Federal funds were identified for the purpose of economic development to upgrade the aging water and sewer lines that were originally installed in the early 1900s. The Vermont legislature needed to provide matching funds of 3 percent while the Town of Waterbury and the then Village (now Edward Farrar Utility District [EFUD]) would need to contribute 2 percent. It took many years of planning, engineering, public meetings, inclusion of other amenities, public acquisition of rights-of-way where needed and final design work.

After many years of design and permitting, the project was put out to bid in 2018, with construction starting in April 2019. Construction was completed in the summer of 2021. The final element will be to remove the remaining utility lines in the core of the downtown in 2022.

The Main Street construction project involved a full replacement of all municipal water and sewer infrastructure, storm drains, roadway and sidewalks. The project included undergrounding of aerial utilities and new traffic signals in the business core of the downtown. New sidewalks, period lampposts, replacement trees and landscaping, informational kiosks, wayfinding signs, hanging flower baskets and banners enhance the entire downtown.

Main Street in downtown Waterbury before the construction project.

Main Street Construction Project showing North Main Street in downtown Waterbury during the long-awaited construction project commencing in April 2019. *Courtesy of Gordon Miller.*

The area of improvement projects starts just east of the railroad bridge by the roundabout and continues for approximately one mile down Main Street toward Middlesex to just before River Road. Utility work, storm drains and sidewalk improvements extended to some of the side streets.

The contractor selected by VTrans through competitive bidding was J.A. McDonald. The owner had local ties to Waterbury and had already completed the Waterbury Roundabout project a few years earlier with great success. The construction project was broken down into four segments that would span the two-and-a-half-year project.

Leading up to and beginning during construction the first year, the community started to see major financial investments by private individuals and businesses to upgrade historic buildings for new businesses and new construction.

As pre-construction plans were taking shape for the second construction season beginning in late March 2020, a new, deadly coronavirus crept into the United States. As of mid-March, the governor signed a "stay-at-home" order and shut down all nonessential activities. The State of Vermont sent all employees statewide home to work remotely, including the state office complex in Waterbury.

The Main Street construction plans were put on hold temporarily while the world and the United States watched as coronavirus, or COVID-19, spread to the East Coast and Vermont and to Waterbury.

During the spring of 2020, the governor declared that some essential businesses such as construction could start work under certain conditions. The traffic flow inconveniences of construction work in the downtown were no longer an issue as in 2019 because most people were working from home and schools were either closed or on remote learning.

A partnership between the town and Revitalizing Waterbury was developed to provide information and support to residents and local businesses during the construction phases. Weekly construction updates were posted on Front Porch Forum, reported on WDEV, printed in the *Waterbury Record* until it ceased operations in March 2020 and then subsequently listed in the online news of the *Waterbury Roundabout*. A website of the construction project was maintained, www.waterburyworks.com. The goal was to communicate, communicate, communicate.

The town received $170,000 in grant funds through the Vermont Downtown Transportation Fund to provide the enhancements that were considered non-participatory enhancements (no federal funds) to complete the Main Street project. These include banners, kiosks, wayfinding signs,

Architectural rendering of the completed Main Street Construction Project.

bike racks, benches, large hanging flower baskets, waste and recycling containers and so on.

The town of Waterbury and EFUD contracted with J.A. McDonald in the spring of 2021 to complete the infrastructure on lower Stowe Street that was not included in the initial Main Street project.

Waterbury has received road and utility improvements to last another fifty to one hundred years. A few key areas like the Stowe Street bridge at the top of Stowe Street still need to be replaced, as that was installed following the flood of 1927 and is considered functionally deficient. Scoping plans are underway for design options for vehicles and pedestrians.

5

WATERBURY VILLAGE DISSOLVED

Edward Farrar Utility District Formed

Skip Flanders

On December 20, 1892, the Waterbury Fire District No. 1 was incorporated as the Village of Waterbury by the Vermont state legislature. This incorporation as a municipal entity allowed the village residents to collect property taxes to pay for services and develop infrastructure within the village boundary. However, town residents would not be taxed for services, including the fire and police departments, the street department, water and sewer systems, streetlights and other amenities. The village government consisted of a village president and two trustees; as the village grew and developed, three water commissioners were added. In 1959, the first vote to merge the town and the village into one town government occurred. Proponents of the merger suggested the merger would lead to a savings in the cost of services. Town residents who would pay higher taxes voted the merger down.

From 1959 to 2011, there were nine merger votes, and all were passed by village voters and defeated by town voters. The sixth merger vote in 2004 was passed by the town but was later voted down on a petition to rescind the previous vote. The town and village governments worked together to consolidate the highway and street departments as well as the fire departments. These consolidations did not require changes in government and resulted in overall savings for Waterbury residents.

The damage from Tropical Storm Irene in 2011 altered the focus of the town and village governments. The municipal office at 51 South Main

Street, owned by the village, was substantially damaged and uninhabitable until there were major repairs. This building housed the town and village offices and the village police department.

The town decided the offices at 51 South Main Street were not adequate for the future and sought a different solution. There were numerous delays in considering the decision of whether to repair the ruined building. Because of damage, the village was forced to rent space for the village police department, which added to the high cost of running this department. The 2016 annual village budget included $334,194 for the police department, which represented 80 percent of the total village budget.

Because of the many failed merger votes, at the 2016 annual village meeting, the trustees were asked to investigate the option of dissolving the village government as an alternative to merger. The trustees prepared an article for the 2017 annual meeting presenting the option of dissolving the village and creating a utility district to own and operate the water and sewer system. This article passed 79 to 13.

The trustees worked with attorney Paul Giuliani to prepare a plan for dissolving the village and creating the Edward Farrar Utility District to continue the care and maintenance of the water and sewer system. Edward Farrar was president of the village trustees and a water commissioner when he was killed in a trench cave-in on October 4, 1904, while installing a sewer line on Elm Street. Naming the utility district after Farrar honored and recognized his service and ultimate sacrifice to his fellow citizens in Waterbury.

The charter of the Edward Farrar Utility District was voted on by village residents by Australian ballot on June 20, 2017, and passed 244 to 83. The charter was then introduced in the 2018 legislative session. The legislature passed the charter dissolving the village and creating the utility district effective July 1, 2018. This ended 135 years of village government and returned the governmental oversight to the Select Board. The last three trustees were Lawrence "Lefty" Sayah and Natalie J. Sherman, with P. Howard "Skip" Flanders, president. The first commissioners of the Edward Farrar Utility District were Robert Finucane, Cindy Parks, Natalie Sherman, Lawrence Sayah and P. Howard Flanders.

Most importantly, there was substantial village voter participation in making this important change to the village government going forward for improved efficiency and making decisions as one community.

PART X

PUBLIC SAFETY

1

VERMONT STATE POLICE PILOT PROJECT

2017–2020

Marc Metayer

Providing police services in Waterbury during the first half of the twentieth century was a divided affair. The Village of Waterbury opted to create and specifically fund a police department to serve the needs of the village district, which at the time had the higher percentage of population and businesses as compared to the rest of Waterbury and Waterbury Center. The expense of the police department was borne by the residents of the village. The police department provided a multitude of local services in a timely fashion with a readily apparent physical presence, albeit limited primarily to the village district.

Upon the establishment of the Vermont State Police (VSP) in 1947, police services were provided to Waterbury without additional financial charges, aside from contributing to state tax revenues. Town residents relied on the rural police services of VSP that provided emergency responses and limited community patrol presence. Given the more rural nature of the town, this arrangement provided satisfactory service for many decades.

As Waterbury entered the twenty-first century, changes to the population distribution and the demands of a vibrant business community prompted serious discussions concerning the viability of supporting a local police department. There were questions, as well, concerning the role of a separate village government. In 2017, village residents voted to eliminate the village trustees and supported a charter change converting the assets of the village into a public utility district. With the elimination of the trustees as a governing body, the police department, which was the last vestige of village services not absorbed previously by the town, became obsolete. The last year of budgeted service by the Village of Waterbury Police Department ended in 2017.

Prior to this time, numerous efforts had been made to encourage town residents to join village residents in supporting a town-wide police department. All efforts failed, as town voters overwhelmingly opposed the proposals. The dissolution of the police department at the end of 2017 prompted a community-wide discussion about the need for police services and how those services could be provided. The town Select Board authorized the formation of a study committee to review the issue of police services and to bring forward recommendations for consideration by the board.

The study committee, composed of volunteers from the resident and business communities within Waterbury, conducted an intensive and expansive review of the issue during the fall of 2017. Background information was gathered from several other Vermont communities comparable to Waterbury in measures of population, geographic size and grand list. This information provided the study committee with a range of options to consider with respect to police department staffing levels, operational expenses, range of services and the effect on the local tax burden.

The study committee focused on four primary points of information to present to the community for consideration:

- What are the demands for police services in Waterbury?
- What is a reasonable level of police services for Waterbury?
- What options are available for the community?
- How would a police department be funded by the community?

Public information meetings were conducted in September and October. The study committee presented background information covering these primary points. In addition to the presentations with question-and-answer sessions, surveys were completed by attendees, allowing the committee to gauge public sentiment. To supplement this feedback, the study committee also used an online survey tool to gather a wider range of community input, ideally from those who may not have been able to attend one of the public information meetings. Community members were presented with three models for providing police services to the Waterbury community:

1. Rely upon the existing resources of the Vermont State Police at the Middlesex Station. This would have no additional tax

burden; however, no dedicated staffing would be provided to Waterbury. This was already in operation.

2. Contract with the Vermont State Police for dedicated services at a level to be determined, requiring direct payments from Waterbury but providing a commitment to patrol presence within the community. This would begin as of July 2018.
3. Establish a town-wide police department with significant impact on the local tax rate along with significant management obligations. This would take years to achieve full implementation.

In November, the study committee presented the research results to the Select Board for consideration. After extensive discussion among Select Board members at public meetings, and with due consideration for comments from community members and the recommendations of the study committee, the Select Board supported a plan to contract for eighty hours per week with the Vermont State Police. The plan would provide for two VSP troopers assigned exclusively to Waterbury, with each providing forty hours per week of patrol coverage, during both day and evening shifts. The Middlesex Station would continue to cover service calls when the assigned troopers were unavailable.

A special town meeting was held in January 2018 for voter approval to fund the police services contract, beginning July 1. Timing for consideration, authorization and institution of the contract, as well as the anticipated level of community discussion of the matter, contributed to the decision to hold the special town meeting in January rather than waiting until the annual town meeting in March. Funding was approved by voters with a decisive voice vote.

The contract for police services in Waterbury represented a pilot project for the community and for the Vermont State Police. This was the first time since 1980–81 that the Vermont State Police had contracted in this fashion for police services with a community. Although the state police provided a variety of overtime contracts with numerous communities over the years and some short-term enforcement contracts, the scale of the model used in the Waterbury project had not been a standard practice for the state police. Waterbury represented the opportunity to test the viability of the model for possible replication in other Vermont communities. The three-year length of the contract was designed to provide an adequate test period to fully evaluate the concept.

The troopers assigned to Waterbury spend the bulk of their assigned shifts patrolling the entire community. Modest office space has been provided at the fire stations, and the visible presence of policing is more consistent than what prevailed over the last few years. Although troopers do not perform all the community caretaking services of a local police department, they do have much greater contact with community members than what would have been the case with coverage solely from the Middlesex station.

One of the notable items of concern identified by the study committee, call response time, has been significantly improved with the inception of the contract. Traditional coverage from the Middlesex station often had response times ranging from thirty minutes to over an hour, depending on the nature of an individual call. The troopers assigned to Waterbury have response times averaging from one to fifteen minutes, depending on the type and location of a call. Prior to the contract implementation, not only were police responses slower, but it was also not unusual for delays to be measured in days rather than minutes. This proved to be a significant point of dissatisfaction with the prior arrangement for police services. Although not completely resolved by the contract, this concern has seen marked improvement.

The Waterbury municipal manager and the Middlesex station commander are the respective official points of contact for monitoring the progress of the pilot project. Monthly statistical reporting is provided for the Select Board, and the information is posted on the town's website for public review. The purpose of the reporting is to monitor the service demands in the community as well as to assess the effect of the police services provided over the longer term.

The Waterbury pilot project with the Vermont State Police was designed as a timely and prudent solution to providing police services throughout the entire community. The community had a sense of urgency due to the dissolution of the village-based police department, and this project provided a bridging opportunity to allow for future community deliberations. Although initially viewed as a temporary option in lieu of establishing a local, town-wide police department, the project has been well accepted by the community and appears to serve the purposes of both Waterbury and the Vermont State Police.

2

WATERBURY AMBULANCE SERVICE INC.

Brian Lindner

The year 2020 saw Waterbury Ambulance Service Inc. (WASI) looking for a location to construct a new building for the squad. Modern ambulances have become larger, and the next generation will no longer fit into the existing building on Guptil Road. At the same time, WASI continues to respond to an average of two emergency calls every day. From 1971 until 2006, WASI depended purely on volunteers to staff the ambulances and manage the administrative work other than the billing, which was handled by a contractor. Until 2002, a "red phone" system answered all telephone calls requesting an ambulance. Up to ten telephones were in volunteers' residences, and calls were answered 24/7. In the mid-1990s, the municipal offices took over "red phone" duties during business hours, as daytime volunteers could no longer be found. In 2001, Capital West took over dispatch duties in Montpelier; this service continues to the current day. During the next several years, WASI paid the Capital West costs. With an increasing call volume, dramatically increased training requirements, declining number of volunteers and a more complex and expensive business environment, in 2006 WASI took the step of hiring John Kueffner of Waterbury Center to become the squad's first paid employee. Kueffner was responsible for responding to emergency calls and running the daily business of the squad. Coupled with all of this, MediCare reimbursements did not keep up with expenses, and WASI's finances became strained. In 2006, the municipality began to pay Capital West for fire and ambulance dispatching although WASI reimbursed the town for its share. At the time, the total dispatching cost for fire and ambulance was $10,000.

By 2009, dispatching costs had risen to nearly $37,000, of which WASI paid $24,000. By 2014, WASI could no longer afford to cover its share without draining its assets. Costs had begun to overtake its nonprofit ability to be self-sustaining. It was in 2014 that the Town of Waterbury began paying for all dispatching costs for both fire and ambulance. Costs for this service rose to over $80,000 during 2020. After forty-three years, residents of Waterbury were finally called upon to help fund the nonprofit squad beyond providing a headquarters building and red phone support. Faced with increasing costs, in 2019 the Towns of Waterbury, Duxbury and Moretown approved budgets that included payments to WASI in proportion to their number of emergency calls. Waterbury's share was nearly $40,000.

One of the primary reasons for increased expenses has been a dramatic decline in volunteers as experienced by ambulance squads across the country. The gaps have been filled with paid staff, most of whom come to WASI to serve on a per diem basis. Michelle Franklin was hired as the second full-time employee and was replaced by Maggie Burke in November 2020 when Franklin left for a new position. Mark Podgwaite is the current executive director, replacing John Kueffner upon his retirement in 2018. Dramatically increased requirements to obtain and maintain an EMT (and higher) certification have been a clear roadblock to recruit new volunteers. EMTs who have gone to great personal expense and time to obtain certification expect to be reimbursed for their skills and expertise.

Currently, WASI has two fully stocked and equipped ambulances, one of which has four-wheel drive. The equipment alone on each rig is measured in tens of thousands of dollars. Modern ambulances are so much larger than Waterbury's 1983 building—the overhead doors must be opened so that the EMTs can walk around to the other side of each ambulance. The Waterbury Backcountry Rescue Team is part of WASI, and its vehicles and gear are housed temporarily in the Maple Street fire station in Waterbury Center.

During the fall of 2020, WASI became an official testing location during the COVID-19 pandemic, and this provided critical funding as the number of emergency calls dropped. As of this writing, the squad is also preparing to become a vaccination site. This too will become a revenue source to support the squad. As part of WASI's efforts, it also runs multiple COVID-19 testing sites in surrounding communities.

Due to preventative procedures and heavy use of personal protective equipment, no EMT at WASI contracted COVID-19 during the first year of the pandemic.

3

WATERBURY BACKCOUNTRY RESCUE TEAM

Brian Lindner

In May 1994, Waterbury Ambulance Service created an informal team of EMTs who were experienced hikers. It was decided the ambulance and duty crew would remain in quarters while the informal team (along with the fire department) would respond to backcountry calls. The goal was to keep the ambulance and crew in town until the patient had been evacuated to a trailhead.

Over the next eight years to October 15, 2001, the number of calls continued to increase, with a total of ten rescues—all on Camels Hump. Each call emptied Waterbury of firefighters. During two nights in 2001, rescues on Camels Hump were run by non-Waterbury agencies. Both rescues were poorly coordinated and tied up eight agencies for all-night rescues.

Dale Jones from the Waterbury Fire Department then took the initial steps to create a specialized backcountry rescue team that would take on the responsibility for the rescue of sick and injured persons in the geographic area covered by Waterbury Fire and WASI. He and others from the ambulance considered how best to take the concept forward. Unfortunately, Jones then passed away, and an ad hoc committee took over the efforts to organize. Several members of the fire department and ambulance formed the initial team. Interestingly, not once during the organizational meetings was the topic of searches for missing persons in the backcountry mentioned. The concentration was purely on the rescue of the sick and injured.

In a vote on April 18, 2002, with Stan Chase as chair, the WASI trustees unanimously approved the creation of the Waterbury Backcountry Rescue Team (WBRT) under WASI and provided all the needed funds to purchase equipment. (Neil van Dyke from the Stowe Hazardous Terrain Team met with WBRT to recommend the gear that should be purchased, and all his recommendations were followed.)

Two months later, on June 24, 2002, WBRT was called out for its first official rescue. A forty-seven-year-old female hiker from Pennsylvania fractured her ankle at the junction of the Monroe and Alpine trails on Camels Hump, near the summit. Only three agencies were needed, with WBRT in command at the Duxbury trailhead. Thirty-seven rescuers responded, and in only four hours and eight minutes from the time of call, the patient was successfully brought to the base. The Waterbury Fire Department remained fully staffed throughout the rescue. Although the operation proceeded smoothly, a list of twenty-three "learning points" was created, detailing ways the next rescue could be improved.

In 2002, WBRT's first year of operation, a total of five rescues were completed. One-half of them were SARs—search and rescues. These were searches for lost persons in the backcountry. Although never discussed during the entire time it took to create the team, SARs quickly came to account for about 50 percent of all WBRT calls and has continued as such throughout the years.

During the first seven years of the team's existence, they responded to about four missions per year. Then in 2010, the number of calls increased. This growth can be directly tied to the increase in the number of cellphones carried by hikers. When hikers could connect with 911, they did. There were twelve calls in 2010, twenty in 2013 and nineteen in 2015.

The calls often came in when the hiker's cellphone battery was down to 10 percent or less, as they had used the flashlight function to negotiate the trail during darkness. Almost without exception, the hikers became lost, injured or ill late in the day and were utterly unprepared for the cold and darkness. In fact, the vast bulk of all WBRT calls have been partly conducted during the night.

Because of a badly executed SAR when a young hiker (Levi Duclos in Ripton on January 9, 2012) died before a proper mission was launched, the Vermont legislature began to tinker with SAR laws. It was at this time that WBRT stopped charging for rescues; the consideration within government and key SAR teams was that these missions should be free to those being rescued regardless of decisions that caused them to require rescue. The fear was that if SARs were billed, people needing rescue would wait until the situation was so horrible, they had no choice but to call. WBRT was the last agency in Vermont to bill for SAR services. (During the COVID-19 pandemic, WASI amended its billing: if a person is in terrain officially designated as closed and required the services of WBRT, they would be billed. No such incident has occurred as of this writing.)

Individuals requiring rescue on extremely hot days are routinely treated for hypothermia. On a very hot day, it can become quite cold when the sun goes down, and if the person has no extra clothing, they get cold quickly. This is further complicated by lying on the ground for hours as rescuers assemble and hike to their location with all the required gear.

WBRT currently owns a truck, a trailer, two all-terrain vehicles and a "snowbulance," which is a trailer towed behind a snowmobile or ATV. The patient and the EMT providing care can ride in this protected from the elements. All vehicles and gear are housed in the Maple Street Fire Station courtesy of the Waterbury Fire Department. During its first twenty years, WBRT responded to a total of 225 missions.

4
WATERBURY FIRE DEPARTMENT

Gary Dillon

The Waterbury Fire Department (WFD) responds to about every type of incident you can think of, ranging from smoke and carbon monoxide alarms, vehicle crashes, building fires and everything in between. When people have a problem and do not know who to call, they call 911, and many of those calls go to the fire department.

From 2000 to 2020, WFD responded to 237 structure fires, not all of which were in Waterbury. As a member of Capital Fire Mutual Aid, we respond at the request of any other departments, as other fire departments come to our aid, upon request. Every fire is devastating to the owner(s), but below are some larger ones to which we responded:

DECEMBER 29, 2002 | The main building of the Gateway Motel on South Main Street experienced a fire that was so devastating the building was taken down and rebuilt to its current structure.

JUNE 2, 2003 | A house fire took the life of a young girl. The fire, heat and smoke had clear movement throughout the house, as many of the doors had been removed for remodeling. Firefighters made an initial attempt using a ladder into a second-story window but had to back down due to a live powerline about to fall from the house onto the ladder that the members were climbing. They came down just before the line fell—it would have electrocuted them. Another window was used and the girl removed. She lived for about twenty-four hours before losing her battle.

January 27, 2005 | In the early morning, a fire broke out at Lydia's Smoke House on Route 100 just past True Value. This building also housed Coffin's repair shop and a pizza shop. Upon arrival, there were flames forty feet in the air. The building was a total loss. Aside from the -20° temperatures, firefighters had to be aware of large vegetable cans exploding and flying through the opening in the roof and landing around the scene.

Later that morning, the WFD received a call for a house fire off Crossett Hill in Duxbury. Members at the station, taking a break to warm up and eat, cut down on the response time and enabled them to keep the fire contained to the originating wall.

February 17, 2014 | The WFD responded to mutual aid in Warren for a condominium complex fire. The entire twenty-four-unit complex was destroyed and had to be taken down. The complex was older and had limited fire stops in the attic, making it difficult to stop.

April 1, 2018 | Although all fires with personal property loss are devastating, the fire at the Wallace farm on Blush Hill hit the community and surrounding communities very hard. The family farmhouse belonging to Rosina Wallace and her brother Kay "Wally" Wallace had been operated for 150 years by five generations. Although Rosina and Wally as well as a dog were not injured, twenty-three cows perished. Anyone who grew up or had lived in Waterbury knew of and likely visited the Wallace farm. The working farm, attached farmhouse and another unattached house were not saved.

The department responds to serious vehicle crashes where sometimes people receive life-changing injuries or lose their lives. In 2020, the department responded to two fatal crashes. One of the individuals who lost her life was a Vermont State Police dispatcher and worked for Montpelier Police as a dispatcher, having dispatched many of the fire departments in central Vermont, including Waterbury.

Of course, members are changed by these incidents. The most vulnerable are those who respond to their first fatal incident, where even the most experienced member is affected. Everyone handles these situations differently, and as a team we work with members to help.

Merger of Two Departments

During the process of working toward two new fire stations in Waterbury, it was clear the two fire departments (Waterbury Village and Town of Waterbury) needed to officially merge into one department. They had been responding and training as one for a few years; it was past time to officially merge. This process started with a meeting between the two fire chiefs, municipal manager, board of trustees and Select Board. The residents of the village needed to vote for a charter change that would eliminate the requirement for a fire department, and the town residents needed to vote to accept the indebtedness and property of the village department.

Although one might think merging two similar departments would be easy, the only easy part was getting the residents of the village and town to support the merger. The challenge was getting forty-plus members to agree how the merger would happen. Each respective "association" had funds to be merged as well as association possessions. Each department had a fire chief, assistant chiefs and line officers (captains and lieutenants). How we adjust the officers, where there are two sets, into one would be the challenge. The town fire chief, David Jennison, and village chief Gary Dillon met several times before having meetings with the entire membership.

As Chief Jennison was the senior fire chief, it was his decision if he wanted to be the chief of the merged department, and this was supported by Chief Dillon. Chief Jennison chose to step down into the first assistant chief position and stayed there for a few years to help work out the wrinkles of merger. Chief Dillon became chief, and the other assistant chiefs took one step down to a new position of battalion chief.

It took a couple years to work out the difference in processes each department had. Emergency scene operations did not change, as we had been responding as one for several years. Today, Waterbury has one of the largest and best departments in the area. We are appropriately equipped, with great support from the residents.

New Stations

A committee worked for a few years on everything from station design to locations. We met with three different prospective contractors to review their designs. After much research to include the number of stations, response times and other associated topics, the location for the new stations would remain the same as the previous locations.

In 2009, a bond vote was approved and withstood a rescission vote. As we were building on existing sites, the apparatus at the Maple Street Station went to the Town Highway Garage and the Vermont National Guard allowed us to place apparatus at the Waterbury Armory.

After a few years of planning and a year of construction, the unveiling of the new stations happened on July 23, 2011. The Main Street Station design required flood proofing, to include concrete walls around the entire building, placing most power above the concrete walls and flood traps that allowed water to enter the building and move throughout to prevent pressure damage. The station's generator was placed on a concrete pedestal, and the apparatus doors were designed with sensors to open when a certain level of water was reached. Who would have thought that about a month after occupying the building, this system of flood proofing would be tested?

Tropical Storm Irene Flooding

Prior to August 28, 2011, many around the region had been paying attention to the weather forecast in anticipation of the possible impact Tropical Storm Irene could have. The evening of August 27, 2011, it began raining in Waterbury; however, it was not more significant than any other rainy night. Even into the following day, the rain in Waterbury was not heavy. The state had been preparing for a bad storm, and flooding around the state, to varying degrees, was anticipated.

Although Waterbury did not receive much rain, upstream on the Winooski and Mad Rivers did, and that water flowed toward Waterbury, merging in Middlesex. The low-lying areas in and around Waterbury had already started to flood, but this sometimes happened, and it was not a large concern.

At about 6:00 p.m. on August 28, things changed dramatically for Waterbury and the surrounding communities. The fire department responded to a car in the water on Route 2 in Moretown; it was then we found that water was across the road and houses were already flooding around the Pines rest area on Route 2 in Waterbury. We returned to the Village to find water was now over the road on the southern end of the village.

Crews were sent from the stations to all streets on the southern end of the village advising people to evacuate to higher ground. After the first sweep, crews went out a second time with the same message. By now, water was coming into the fire station. Members who were there started moving everything they could to the second floor. Soon after, the LP gas to the building and generator was shut down, and everyone evacuated to nearby Bank Hill on Main Street to "stand by."

We returned to the station at 6:30 a.m. the following day as the water was receding. We purchased all the bleach we could locate and started washing the station interior as we pushed water to the storm drains in front of the station.

The station was cleaned, relying on generator power, within three hours. The elevator had to be serviced, and the only item lost was a cabinet in the bathroom. We were fortunate compared to what others in and around Waterbury sustained. Homes were lost due to the flood, including those of two of our members. Other firefighters' homes sustained serious damage. Fortunately, there were no flood-associated deaths in the area.

Paying It Forward

The Waterbury Fire Department has a long history of paying it forward. Outstanding examples of this include:

- Mandy Morse | Firefighter Amanda "Mandy" Morse was born with a genetic liver disease and would eventually need a liver transplant. She suffered a brain aneurysm, which complicated her medical condition. The firefighters hosted a dinner to raise money to send prospective match donors to Minnesota for testing. Two members completed the process but were not a match; a third was being tested when Mandy unfortunately lost her battle. Mandy was a daughter, mother, wife, teacher and sister firefighter. She is missed by all who knew her.
- Rosina and Wally Wallace | After the devastating fire at the Wallace Farm on Blush Hill, members of the department held a dinner, raising over $6,000 to aid the Wallaces, who had lost their livestock and most of the farm buildings and home.
- A young firefighter from Lamoille County was diagnosed with cancer and needed funds for travel and treatment; WFD donated $500.

All pay-it-forward events were funded from the Firefighters' Association and not taxpayer money.

J.A. McDonald Construction Company

The Waterbury Main Street construction finally happened. This was a project that had been planned and canceled many times since the early 1980s. The contractor was J.A. McDonald. They were very responsive to not only the needs of the community during construction but also the Fire Department when we had calls. The Fire Department held a cookout in July 2019 when the J.A. McDonald crew was scheduled to work a half day. All the workers were invited back for lunch.

Year two of the three-year project, the coronavirus created too many restrictions to have another cookout; however, the Fire Department showed its appreciation by distributing over $500 in Waterbury Bucks to J.A. McDonald workers. The Waterbury Bucks could be used like cash in Waterbury businesses. Adding to the fun, the workers were asked to choose an envelope and answer the question on the front—of course, everyone was a winner.

Naturally, much has changed over the past twenty years; however, the commitment of the Waterbury Fire Department to our community has not.

5

WATERBURY VILLAGE POLICE

Natalie Sherman

The Village of Waterbury incorporated on December 20, 1882. From that time forward, the village voted and paid, through village property taxes, to provide improvements for its residents, including police protection. The Waterbury Village Police Department served the municipality, which covered an approximately 1.1-square-mile area of Waterbury's downtown and surrounding residential and commercial properties.

Waterbury Village had two police chiefs spanning the years from 2000 to 2020. William Wolfe served from 1999 to 2007, and Joby Feccia, promoted from Waterbury Village police officer to police chief in 2008, until the village was dissolved in 2017, eliminating the police department.

William Wolfe joined the Village Police Department as interim chief of police in the autumn of 1999. Prior to his employment as chief of police in Waterbury, he served at the Barre Police Department. He replaced Waterbury's Chief Doug Howe, who resigned after having served for four years. In March 2000, Interim Chief Wolfe was appointed chief of police.

The police department employed both full-time and part-time officers. Chief Wolfe's focus was to build a community policing department to work as a team with citizens to combat crime. He stated, "In order to be effective, a police department must be interactive with the community it serves, so that together we can keep Waterbury a safe place to live." He enjoyed visiting businesses and staying in contact with owners, residents and visitors. During Chief Wolfe's tenure, the community welcomed police officer foot and bicycle patrols. The department also continued the traditions of supporting the Toys for Tots program and celebrating with families while handing out glow sticks and candy at Halloween. Also important to the community was the annual Bicycle Safety Program for children. With the support of the village trustees, the Village Police Department renamed the Bicycle Safety Program the Wayne Sourdiff Bike Rodeo in honor of former chief Wayne Sourdiff, who passed away in 1995 while in service as chief of police.

While the village supported the police department, the challenge of maintaining a full-time force was appreciable. Having a full-time police department was expensive. The Village Police Department served the village with limited pay-for-service coverage to the town. With no agreement from the town for paying up front for service, providing consistent service was a challenge.

Under the leadership of Chief Feccia, the police department continued to maintain traditions of working with programs important to the community: providing safety measures at NQID celebrations, celebrating with families on Halloween, participating in annual Independence Day celebrations, Safety Day events, the Waterbury Community Fair, leading traffic and pedestrian safety during annual Leaf Peepers races and hosting the volunteers of the Wayne Sourdiff Child Safety Foundation's Wayne Sourdiff Bike Rodeo. Chief Feccia enjoyed and believed it was important to support youth programs such as the Everybody Wins! mentoring program at the Thatcher Brook Elementary School and being a Boy Scout leader.

Chief Feccia continued roles he held when he was an officer: DARE program instructor and maintaining child safety seat installation certification. Supporting the training of officers was a priority. Maintaining training and preparation for the protection of his officers and the betterment of public safety were important to the chief, and he paid careful attention to and implemented extensive and varied officer training and courses such as First Aid, Domestic Violence, Vermont Criminal Law, Vermont Motor Vehicle Law, Responding to Mental Health Crises, Use of Narcan, rifle training and twenty-first-century training.

Over the next few years, the police department experienced recurring challenges. It was difficult to retain qualified people, and officer turnover was costly. It was expensive to send officer candidates to school for qualification, and once hired, there was little opportunity for advancement within a small police department. The Village Police Department saw many officers come and go, seeking opportunities for advancement elsewhere. Along with cost pressures of staffing and managing a police department, several other economic challenges resonated in our community.

The Dale Correctional Facility for Women closed in 2009, and revenues from the Department of Corrections ended, cutting into the village budget with an annual loss of roughly $40,000. Ostensibly, that revenue source was used to offset police services in the village. In 2011, Tropical Storm Irene intensified strains on the police department, reducing property values and the grand list. This caused property taxes to rise significantly even when the operating budget was held level. To relieve the tax burden, operating budget cuts were necessary, and as the police department commanded most of the village's budget, the department was hit hard.

With operating budget reductions, reduced shifts and coverage assistance by the Vermont State Police, the Village Police Department refocused on essential services with less emphasis on community and quality-of-life policing. Growing frustration took a toll, and the community realized the small population of the village couldn't afford the tax rate for policing to adequately provide the necessary and desired services.

At the March 2011 Village Meeting, there were discussions about the ability of the village to support a police department. A motion passed reducing the police budget. Later, at a special meeting in April, the budget was restored, highlighting that reduced costs could not sustain a department beyond the minimum required expenses. This called attention to the need for other measures such as town merger, local option tax funding or that which later occurred—dissolution of the village, which would need agreement by the village voters.

In August 2011, the village's municipal office at 51 South Main Street was destroyed by Tropical Storm Irene. A new location for the police department and municipal offices needed to be found. In 2012, the town and village worked to create the first proposal for a new municipal complex, which included space for the police department on the Stanley/Wasson Hall site at the state's office complex. The village agreed to contribute $500,000 to include the police department in this project if approved by town voters. This proposal failed at a bond vote in June 2013; there was little support from the town to include space for the police department in the next municipal complex design. The exemption was another important strain on the police department. Space was rented for the Village Police Department at the Steele Block at 46 South Main Street.

In addition to managing the police department operations, 2012 saw a lawsuit filed against the village in a dispute over the termination of Officer

Adam Hubacz. The case continued in the courts until December 2018, with a conclusion confirming the lawful termination. Though insurance covered much of the legal expenses, the village spent $117,700, plus untold staff time, matriculating the case through the courts.

Due to concerns with management of the police department, including a request for an investigation into allegations of misconduct within the Village Police Department at the 2012 Annual Village Meeting and motions to reduce the police department budget in both 2011 and 2012, the trustees asked by Australian ballot if the voters wanted to maintain the Village Police Department. Despite the majority vote in November 2012 expressing the choice to continue with the police department, concerns about police services continued. The completion of the management evaluation investigation remained pending awaiting the resolution of the termination lawsuit.

During this time, police patrolling and services continued with some notable heroic service. In 2013, during a routine traffic stop, long-serving officer Anthony Mazzilli was faced with a car operator locking himself in their car, wielding a knife and slashing his neck. Mazzilli responded swiftly using tools to open the car door and applied lifesaving measures to the operator. The car operator later reached out to Officer Mazzilli with gratitude. Chief Feccia presented Officer Mazzilli with a Life Savings Award on behalf of the Waterbury Village Police Department.

At the 2016 village meeting, attendees asked the Trustees to investigate the option of dissolving the Village to accomplish what the previous failed merger votes were unable to do and to create one government for Waterbury. At the village's 2017 annual meeting, an article directed the trustees to draft amendments to the village charter that would eliminate most general government functions, including police services. It was approved by voters. The trustees worked with attorney J. Paul Giuliani regarding these proposed amendments, and the trustees voted to hold a special meeting vote on June 20, 2017. That vote to amend the charter of the village, dissolving the village (along with the police department) was approved by an Australian ballot, 224 in favor, 83 opposed.

The Vermont state legislature approved the dissolution of the village through passage of H.716. After receiving the governor's signature, the Village of Waterbury dissolved on July 1, 2018. It was succeeded by the Edward Farrar Utility District.

The Village Police Department prepared for closure of operations at the end of 2017. In a special town meeting on January 23, 2018, residents voted to enter a contract with the state's Department of Public Safety to provide police services by having two state troopers work in Waterbury a total of eighty hours a week.

Waterbury is a better community because of the contributions of the village residents, elected and appointed village officials and the services of the Waterbury Village Police Department. With the close of the village government, the residents of Waterbury proceed together as one community. The Waterbury village and town residents owe a debt of gratitude to all who have served and worked cooperatively to bring Waterbury to this point in history.

PART XI

RECREATION

1

FRIENDS OF WATERBURY RESERVOIR

Friends of Waterbury Reservoir Board Members Walter Carpenter, Sheila Goss and Francine Chittenden and President Eric Chittenden

In 1994, the Friends of Waterbury Reservoir (Friends) was born of a need to address user conflicts. The Friends of Waterbury Reservoir is committed to protecting and enhancing the ecological, historical, recreational and community values of the Waterbury Reservoir. The vision of the Friends is that the Waterbury Reservoir be a thoughtfully maintained, safe and clean public-access recreation area located at the crossroads of world-class resort towns while offering a remote outdoor experience for users. The Waterbury Reservoir is recognized as a unique resource and important conservation and economic asset for the people of Vermont.

The Waterbury Reservoir was drawn down in November 2000 to complete major repair work to the dam's center section and for bank stabilization work. This drawdown remained in effect until the spring of 2007. During that time, Waterbury Center State Park (WCSP) and the Cotton Brook canoe access were closed. Naturally, usage on the reservoir decreased, and recreational expectations segued to more biking, hiking and camping. The Friends organization was mostly dormant during this time. Although there was ongoing dialogue between the board and various state agencies regarding these repairs, there were few formal meetings of the Friends.

When the reservoir was refilled to its normal 860-acre level, visitors, surface users and anglers returned in greater numbers than ever. Other important returnees included loons, eagles, hawks, herons and other wildlife. In a few short years, the Waterbury Reservoir went from a relatively unknown recreational area to one of the busiest recreational bodies of water within the Vermont borders.

People come to the reservoir, not just from the local area, but from all over Vermont, across the nation, from Canada and around the world. The largest numbers of regular Vermont visitors come from Chittenden, Lamoille, Washington and Franklin Counties. Waterbury Center State Park (WCSP), for example, has gone from about 20,000 visits per season before the reservoir was drained in 2000 to 45,000 visits in recent years. WCSP now ranks as one of the busiest day-use parks in Vermont. Vermont's Department of Forest, Parks and Recreation State extended its season until Indigenous People's Day in mid-October. Additionally, Little River Campground is one of the state park system's busiest, with about 45,000 visitors annually. Over twenty remote campsites around the reservoir add about 7,000 visitors. The surprise user group is the combination of all users who do not check in with any tracking system; they usually park at unsupervised parking areas around the lake, but often they are simply dropped off. Estimates are paddleboarders (3,500), motorboaters (3,500), paddlers and kayakers (5,500), anglers (4,000), water-skiers (1,500) and swimmers (250). These estimates total over 18,000, bringing the total estimated annual users to 115,000. This increased usage has made it necessary to hire a designated special ranger on the water to monitor these recreational resources, especially the remote campsites.

There are many reasons for the reservoir's use to explode. One, of course, is its breathtaking beauty. Another is the growing list of troubles that Lake Champlain and other neighboring bodies of water have been experiencing over the last several years, such as nonnative and invasive encroachment and usage pressure. Another reason is Waterbury and Stowe's rapid population growth over recent years. The rapid evolution of the paddle-sports industry has also made the reservoir a magnet location for these new solo recreational crafts that enjoy more protected, calmer waters.

As the reservoir gained popularity, some of the problems of the past returned and gained steam. These problems included the degradation of shoreline, overuse and unregulated use occasionally resulting in user conflicts. *Brittle naiad*, an invasive species, became established in many parts of the lake. In 2015, the Friends of Waterbury Reservoir rose to the occasion and decided to initiate a greeter program designed to limit further spread of this and other invasive species. This "meet, greet and inform" program utilizes

Enthusiastic group paddlers enjoying the Waterbury Reservoir at Little River State Park during the summer. *Courtesy of Sheila Goss.*

paid staff and volunteers to educate the public about how these invasive species spread via the transportation of watercraft between infested lakes and ponds onward to the reservoir. The Friends of Waterbury Reservoir trains, pays for and insures staff to staff the greeter program.

From 2013 until 2017, Laurie (Smith) Keve served as president of the Friends of Waterbury Reservoir and helped strengthen the organization by developing a new board of directors and clarifying a mission, vision and values. Laurie brought her nonprofit, organizational and social media skills to the Friends and initiated several new projects. Some of these projects include the Boat Access Greeter Program, the Rozalia Project (trash clean-up), developing a social media and website presence and obtaining nonprofit status.

In 2017, John Bauer took over the reins as president. John's leadership and technical skills brought finesse to the organization. Under his guidance, the Friends systematized the greeter program; hosted annual meetings; crafted grant proposals; started the Reservoir loon recovery and protection program; and strengthened state, local and organizational partnerships.

The Waterbury Reservoir has reached a turning point in the history of its usage. It cannot return to the years before 2000. It must evaluate how to manage the explosive growth while balancing the lake's growing popularity and multiple uses without destroying the environment and the incredible wildlife habitat. The Friends of Waterbury Reservoir knows that this will not be easy. For example, with so many new users coming to the reservoir, there have been traffic jams at the Blush Hill Access, at the dam and cars lining up at the WCSP. Long lines of cars waiting to get into these areas occurred on busy days. The Friends must also continue to expand and manage the greeter program to keep invasive species at bay. If milfoil or some other invasive were to take hold, it could very quickly affect the environmental, recreational and economic benefits of the Reservoir. Going into 2021, these challenges to the Reservoir will only increase, and the Friends will be on the front lines.

Small organizations like the Friends of Waterbury Reservoir are born because of a passionate, targeted interest. The Waterbury Reservoir is an incredibly beautiful lake that was created as an answer to disaster. Following the flood of 1927, the dam was constructed as a tool for flood control. Generation of power was incorporated into the original design. That was the early 1930s. In 1963, recreation was added to the list of management uses of the lake. All who appreciate this gem called the Waterbury Reservoir must give deference to the history and priorities of its creation. Many of our goals are being met, thanks to the tireless help of both past and current board members: Laurie (Smith) Keve, John Bauer, Chuck Kletecka, Francine Chittenden, Steve Brownlee, Emma Brownlee, Fred Abraham, Sheila Goss, Faith Beiler, Steve Winters, Eric Chittenden and many others. Our work comes from the heart and a special caring for the natural environment in which we are fortunate to be living.

2

VERMONT FORESTS, PARKS AND RECREATION'S MANAGEMENT OF THE WATERBURY RESERVOIR

Susan Bulmer, Northeast Regional Parks manager, Vermont Department of Forests, Parks and Recreation

At the turn of the twenty-first century, the Waterbury Reservoir was sixty-two years old. The Little River valley near the Ricker Mountain basin was flooded when the Waterbury Dam was completed in 1938, creating the approximately nine-hundred-acre pool.

Although the dam was built primarily for flood control and prevention, it also generates an average fifteen million kilowatt-hours of electric energy each year. The dam is nearly two thousand feet long and about two hundred feet high. The reservoir it creates is a Y-shaped body of water that is five miles long, measured from its most distant points, and averages eighty to one hundred feet deep. The created fifteen miles of shoreline, almost entirely undeveloped, are surrounded by over forty-four thousand wilderness acres of the Mount Mansfield State Forest.

To protect the dam from failing, a large project to repair the dam occurred in the early 2000s when most of the reservoir was drained. The resulting repair work started in July 2000 and took approximately seven years, during which time the Waterbury Center State Park was left dry and was not operated as a day-use beach. Waterbury Center Park attendance went from 23,413 in 1999 to 5,821 in 2000 to 0 from 2001 to 2006. Attendance bounced back quickly to 19,795 in 2007 once the water returned and has increased ever since to 36,990 park visitors in 2019. Little River State Park also had a decrease in over half its overall attendance during the same period

(36,818 in 1999 to 13,888 in 2005). Little River attendance has increased dramatically since the water in the reservoir returned and as the mountain bike system has been developed. In 2019, park attendance at Little River State Park was 45,215 park visitors.

The Waterbury Dam's flood control has been utilized often during the twenty-first century, most notably during the damaging Tropical Storm Irene in 2011, when nearly five inches of rain fell on the region. By holding back much of the resulting flood's impact from the Little River, the Waterbury Dam and Reservoir spared the village of Waterbury and other downstream areas from greater Irene damage.

During a period of sudden snowmelt followed by significant rains in the spring of 2019, a major landslide occurred half a mile inland from the Little River reservoir's confluence of Cotton Brook, a major contributing tributary to the reservoir. After approximately twelve acres of forest sloughed off and struck the Cotton Brook, it was washed into the reservoir, resulting in massive sedimentation and subsequent clouding of the water. At the time of this writing, the landslide area remains a potentially hazardous site, per the Vermont Geological Society.

With regular water levels and fair conditions, recreation on the water and surrounding shoreline has always been popular. Two of the state's most popular parks are on the reservoir: Waterbury Center State Park is used by the public as a beach and boat launch while Little River State Park is one of Vermont's largest campgrounds. It also boasts excellent hiking and biking trails. The Waterbury Reservoir itself is a diverse recreational destination where users can enjoy boating, angling, water skiing, swimming, hiking, camping, hunting, ice fishing, snowmobiling and cross-country skiing. The Vermont Department of Forests, Parks and Recreation (DFPR) has systematically expanded its protection management in keeping with increased use of this beautiful asset.

While management and oversight of the water's surface was more precisely defined by the Vermont Water Resource Board in 1994, the management plan for the use of the reservoir's remote shoreline wasn't created by DFPR until 2012, in response to an observed significant increase in camping and day use. The public were using paddle craft and motorboats to access popular campsites that were spread around the reservoir's shoreline.

Largely unmanaged, these campsites were beginning to show signs of negative wear through increased usage. Trees were being damaged, human waste was not being properly disposed of and campfires were built in dangerous locations. Campsites were being claimed by individual

Winter scene at the Waterbury Reservoir in the Little River State Park, capturing a view of the Green Mountains. *Courtesy of Vermont Department of Forests, Parks and Recreation.*

groups for extended periods while lawn furniture, BBQ grills, abandoned camping gear and general litter were observed along the shoreline and in the reservoir's waters.

During the years of 2011 through 2015, with public input and while working with the volunteer organization, Friends of Waterbury Reservoir, the DFPR enacted a gradual management of the remote campsites and day-use areas on the shorelines. Campsites were identified that were studied to be above the flood line, with safe placement for campfires, ease of access by boat and suitable locations for future sanitary facilities. Similarly, day-use areas were identified where users could enjoy shore activities from dawn to dusk.

A position was created for a dedicated parks staff to oversee daily usage of the reservoir. Working from a motor craft, the reservoir park ranger serves as a resource to assist users to responsibly enjoy the resource while overseeing the remote camping. The park ranger (manager), working within the Little River State Park system, also maintains all navigational buoys, helps with upkeep of the boat launches and provides emergency response as needed.

From 2015 to present, the management of the Waterbury Reservoir continues to grow alongside public usage. All twenty-seven remote campsites are numbered, mapped and maintained by parks staff. The Vermont Youth Conservation Corps, working under contract and

Moonglow shot taken from one of the remote campsites at the Waterbury Reservoir, one of many sites in the Little River State Park. *Courtesy of Vermont Department of Forests, Parks and Recreation.*

supervision of DFPR, built a composting toilet structure at every campsite and some selected day-use areas.

Presently, camping on the reservoir's shoreline remains first come, first served, and campers need to complete a basic registration with the park ranger once they have pitched in at a vacant campsite. With increased demand, which peaked during the spring and summer of the COVID-19 pandemic, considerations are underway to implement a reservation system for the reservoir's campsites, in keeping with other popular state parks.

The Waterbury Reservoir is a treasured recreational asset nestled in a beautiful and historic valley. The Vermont Department of Forests, Parks and Recreation is proud to help manage and protect it for future generations to enjoy.

3

WATERBURY AREA TRAILS ALLIANCE (WATA)

Nat Fish and Ryan McGuire

WATA, founded in 2015, maintains twenty trails with a total length of seventeen miles in the Perry Hill and Little River area of Waterbury. Trail users (both visitors and residents) and local businesses supporting them include runners, hikers, mountain bikers, bird watchers, skiers, snowshoers and walkers. The organization is run by volunteers with the commitment to maintain and enhance Waterbury's public trails.

Originally, the Waterbury Trail Network was overseen by the Stowe Mountain Bike Club; however, when that organization dropped out of the Vermont Mountain Bike Association (VMBA), the Perry Hill trails were left without a steward. Several Waterbury community members banded together (including Nat Fish, Jay Provencher, Ian Turkle, Joe Cavalear, Cris Jones, Dana Allen, Alex Showerman, Amanda McKay, Rebecca Washburn, Keith Macchione, Alex King and Shaun Cattanach) and created WATA, under the sponsorship of VMBA.

Since 2015, WATA has added trails and increased maintenance and trail upkeep, making the trail networks in Waterbury known throughout the country. Having access to this amazing resource has increased tourism and made Waterbury a destination for the mountain bike community.

Trail use is skyrocketing, as evidenced by the need for additional parking on River Road, which is the only public access point to the Perry Hill Trails. The Gravel Grinder is a fundraising ride with participation growing from fewer than twenty riders the first year to five hundred riders in 2019. The 2020 race was not held due to the pandemic.

4

WATERBURY UNLEASHED DOG PARK

Anne M. Imhoff

In the early 2000s, the Waterbury Recreation chairman, Gordon Miller, began searching for a site for a leash-free area in Waterbury so dogs could run free, play and socialize. Several locations were considered but rejected for various reasons. When Tropical Storm Irene arrived in 2011, the project was put on hold.

Finally, in 2014, the project was taken up again with the help of the recreation director, Chad Ummel. The village trustees were approached, and they agreed that a space behind the Waterbury Ice Center, part of the old dump site, be used for a dog park. Waterbury Unleashed Dog Park was finally born.

With the help of many volunteers and the town highway department, the area was cleared of bricks, brush, old cement and trees. A Kickstarter campaign, fundraisers, generous donations and grants raised enough money for the purchase of fencing, materials for tables, chairs, a shed, a riding mower, a Facebook page and a sunshade structure. Yestermorrow Architects of Warren agreed to have its summer interns design and erect the sunshade structure in May 2015. Waterbury Unleashed would pay for the prep work and all the materials needed.

Meanwhile, bylaws were written, committee members appointed, building permits obtained and maintenance chores assigned. Jean Snelling, Waterbury Dog Park treasurer, set up a 501(c)(3) account as a place to hold the funds and from which to pay bills.

Lowe's installed fencing around the park area, with double gates for safe access and egress. The town water department installed a water spigot for dogs to have fresh drinking water. Local Boy Scouts cut a trail to the nearby river so the dogs could swim in the summer. Bill Apoa built a picnic table, Adirondack chairs, a bulletin board and a storage shed for the riding mower. Natalie Sherman planted an entrance garden, and Gordon, Chad, Natalie and Steve Lotspeich put the shingles on the roof of the sunshade structure. In August 2015, the Waterbury Unleashed Dog Park officially opened with a festive dog party.

The park has become the favorite location for residents and out-of-towners to bring their dogs to run free. It is the only dog park in central Vermont, as other parks are in the Burlington area. Summer evenings after 5:00 p.m. seem to be the busiest times, as owners who have been at work all day bring their four-legged buddies down to play while they socialize with other owners.

In 2018, a small area of the overall park was fenced in for small dogs that were uncomfortable running with larger dogs. As the Edward Farrar Utility District took over the properties previously owned by the Village of Waterbury, a new Memo of Understanding for the use of the park area was signed. Many of the original volunteers began drifting away, and in 2019 Abby Teel and Ashley Kiel took over general management of the park. A fifth anniversary party was planned for August 2020, but COVID-19 put a stop to that. The dog park will have to wait until Governor Scott turns the spigot all the way on before a large celebration can be held.

PART XII

TOURISM AND HOSPITALITY

1
ALCHEMIST BREWERY

Liz Schlegel

The Alchemist Pub & Brewery opened in downtown Waterbury at the corner of Main and Elm in the building that now houses Prohibition Pig and formerly housed the Waterbury Post Office, built around 1900. In November 2003, cofounders John and Jen Kimmich chose to launch their business in Waterbury because of its friendliness, its location as "Crossroads of Vermont" meant easy access to multiple ski areas and the opportunity they sensed here.

Within weeks (days!), the Alchemist was the most popular spot in town. A combination of great, well-priced food; a variety of delicious house-brewed beers like Holy Cow, Donovan's Red, Pappy's Porter and Lightweight; and friendly, welcoming and professional service brought in both locals and visitors. The business, its success and its relationship with Waterbury only grew and strengthened in the years to come.

Jen and John first met in 1995, when they were both working at the Vermont Pub and Brewery in Burlington. Jen grew up in Barre and John in Pittsburgh, but beer and Vermont brought them together. John was learning the beer trade from craft beer pioneer Greg Noonan, and Jen was waiting tables when they began their journey as a couple, but it wasn't a straight shot from Burlington to opening their own place in Waterbury. They took lots of detours along the way, in tourist meccas like Boston and Jackson Hole, learning the details of brewing, the tricks of the pub trade and the passionate commitment to quality and customer service that is their hallmark. Less than a decade after they met, they had worked, saved and planned—and were ready to open their own place. And luckily, they chose Waterbury.

The Alchemist restaurant located on Main Street in downtown Waterbury, showing happy pub customers. *Courtesy of Gordon Miller.*

In its first years, the Alchemist instantly established itself as a place filled with heart and local pride. Noted M.K. Monley, in giving John and Jen Revitalizing Waterbury's Community Service award in 2014, "When you came to Waterbury with your business, I don't think any of us knew how much you would mean to our community and to us individually. You have embraced Waterbury as your hometown, and for that we are so grateful. You are terrific employers, neighbors, friends and, not least, beer makers. You have built a worldwide reputation and a fanatic fan base, and you've never stopped paying attention to your own backyard."

Who can forget Kenny Gardner behind the bar and on the Not Quite Independence Day Parade float, the "mayor of Waterbury," with the Alchemist himself in his white coat entertaining the crowd each year? John and Jen were everywhere you turned—in the kitchen, in the cellar brewing magical beers, playing pool, checking on customers in the dining room, pouring behind the bar, bringing their little boy Charlie everywhere they went.

They weren't just running their business; they were building community. They were closely connected with community events, hosting events and celebrations, showcasing local art on the pub walls, donating to all kinds of local activities and raising funds for the renovation of the Railroad Station with their Revitalization Rye, which sold out in just a few hours.

And they were winning beer awards regionally, nationally and internationally. John brewed over ninety different beers in the pub, each one available for just a week or two—and sometimes only a day. Year after year, the Alchemist's reputation grew, and after a *New York Times* write-up by Mark Bittman in 2008, it was standing-room-only every day of the week. The beer, the food, the service, the company—together it made for a destination business that brought people to Waterbury to visit and to stay and brought locals pride and joy. The foot traffic from the Alchemist's downtown location helped other local establishments, and Waterbury's reputation as a foodie paradise started to grow.

As the business grew and strengthened, John and Jen started thinking about next steps. John's beer Heady Topper, a fruity double IPA, was a runaway hit with customers. Jen—always looking toward the future and thinking about ways to grow the business—convinced John that it would be a good idea to bottle (in the end it turned out to be cans) this one, very special, beer. Why not give it a try? And so, in 2010 they began looking for a space to run a production line.

Waterbury had been a great place to run their pub, and it was where they wanted to run their cannery. John and Jen found a location on Crossroad, just off Route 100; it had been the former home of the Green Mountain Chocolate Company. This looked like it could work—a small manufacturing plant readily accessible from the highway, with a small retail space, room for stainless brewing barrels and a canning line. Jen got the finances organized and arranged for the building to be fitted up while John started planning the brewing and canning of that one special beer. They were hoping to release Heady Topper to the world in September 2011.

And that's where things stood when Tropical Storm Irene came to Waterbury. It has been written about in so many accounts, this storm of the century that did so much damage to so many homes and businesses and lives, that it need not be described here. To understand how it affected the Alchemist Pub & Brewery, it might be enough to think about their location on the corner of Main and Elm Streets and consider the fact that nearly all Main Street, all of Elm Street and all of Randall Street were disastrously inundated. And consider that their brewing operation was below ground level: the beer, the restaurant, the business, all destroyed. Famously, John went to the pub on that Sunday evening of August 28, 2011, to check on the rising water and poured himself a beer as he stood in waist-high water to toast the ruins of their business.

And yet up the hill stood the new cannery, ready to start rolling cans off the line. In a 2017 *Food & Wine/Longreads* article, John and Jen noted how incredible it was that they were able to start selling beer right away. "People were coming over and buying Heady, and we knew we were at least helping a little bit," John said. "Those were an emotional couple of days. It was wild." "We were able to bump up production there immediately and employ some people from the pub," Jen said. "That was really important to us."'

Though their own successful business was irreparable and their new venture untested, John and Jen threw themselves into helping Waterbury recover from the devastation of Tropical Storm Irene. They organized Oktoberfest downtown to bring people together to celebrate the ongoing recovery and collaborated with California's Stone Brewing on a special brew, Come Hell or High Water, which raised over $116,000 for rebuilding homes.

Employees who were used to tending bar, cooking French fries or waiting tables were learning quickly how to fill cans and sell beer, T-shirts and glassware to customers who were suddenly coming from everywhere. Everyone pitched in and learned new skills, and the little cannery increased production from the 400 barrels of everything that had been brewed at the pub to 1,500 of Heady Topper in the first year. A year later, it was up to 9,000 barrels of Heady.

The launch of Heady Topper was wildly successful and changed the beer industry, not just in Vermont but around the country. The Alchemist's innovative canning approach, as well as the distinctive character of the renowned beer, have been widely noted as having a lasting effect on craft brewing. Hazy IPA has become a worldwide phenomenon and has been recognized as a new style of beer, and Heady Topper is generally accepted as the nexus of this phenomenon.

Waterbury, Vermont, was the only place in the world to buy Heady Topper, and everyone wanted some. Locals and tourists came to the little shop in droves, until—concerned about the crowds of beer tourists and cars spilling onto Route 100—the Vermont Agency of Natural Resources determined that the canning facility's permit did not actually allow retail sales. This was a blow to the slowly regrowing business, but again, as they had before, John and Jen reinvented their business. They started selling through local retail stores and directly to customers in parking lot pop-ups. And, as they had at the pub and at the cannery, the customers came.

The Alchemist Brewery canning line with co-owner John Kimmich canning the ever-popular Heady Topper craft beer. *Courtesy of Gordon Miller.*

In 2016, the Kimmichs opened a second brewery, the Alchemist Brewery and Retail Center, in Stowe, Waterbury's neighbor to the north and a world-famous tourist destination. The opportunity to keep brewing Heady Topper in Waterbury while adding other beers to the mix and selling directly to customers proved another successful way to expand the business. This new venture allowed them the latitude to expand their philanthropy and community activism, and today the Alchemist is a major donor and doer in the communities where its employees live and work, from Duxbury and Waterbury north throughout the Lamoille Valley.

Though the COVID-19 pandemic has curtailed the customer brewery visits that are the heart of the Alchemist's business, it has continued brewing and selling beer, staying connected to the community and shifting to meet the changing demands of the times. The Alchemist continues to be a successful business and a powerful force for good in Waterbury.

Heady Topper is still brewed in the cannery off Crossroad in Waterbury. Nine thousand barrels a year of this sought-after beer are now distributed throughout Vermont and the United States, delighting customers who can enjoy this special beer, helping retailers stay open in hard times and keeping people employed right here in town.

The future is unpredictable, but one thing that we know is that Jen and John will keep innovating and keep making every shift they need to keep the Alchemist strong and their employees thriving, even as they create joy and community.

2

BEN & JERRY'S

Laura Peterson

The start of the twenty-first century opened a new chapter for Ben & Jerry's. The ice cream company, started in Burlington in 1978 by two junior high school friends in a renovated gas station, had grown to be a multimillion-dollar brand and a part of the cultural conversation. Now it drew the attention of one of the world's largest multinational corporations.

Unilever, a global consumer goods company, acquired Ben & Jerry's in April 2000, despite the cofounders' desire to remain independent. The purchase agreement included several important conditions, including the establishment of an independent board of directors responsible for the company's brand integrity, product quality and social mission. Perhaps even more important to the people of Waterbury, the agreement prohibited layoffs and benefits cuts for two years.

It was a rocky marriage at first—a joining of two companies of vastly different size, temperament and culture. But the power of Ben & Jerry's values-led, mission-driven business model combined with innovative flavors and outrageous creativity was undeniable. The Waterbury factory, along with a factory in St. Albans, continued to churn out surprising fan favorites like the homage to TV's *Seinfeld*—Festivus: A Flavor for the Rest of Us.

Even more popular were the pints created to highlight a social issue or support a cause. One Sweet Whirled (2002) was a partnership with the Dave Matthews Band and SaveOurEnvironment.org to help fight global warming. Primary Berry Graham (2004) was created with Rock the Vote to

Ben & Jerry's sign located on Route 100 in Waterbury, welcoming tourists to enjoy a tour of the world-renowned ice cream manufacturing facility. *Courtesy of Ben & Jerry's.*

drive voter turnout among young people. And to protest oil drilling in the Arctic National Wildlife Refuge, the company constructed a nine-hundred-pound baked Alaska on the U.S. Capitol lawn with Fossil Fuel ice cream.

Meanwhile, the Waterbury plant continued to delight ice cream lovers with its factory tour, colorful scoop shop, Winter Fests and summer movies. The factory quickly became Vermont's number one tourist destination, attracting 350,000 people a year. Many came to visit the "dearly de-pinted" in the Flavor Graveyard, a final resting place for flavors that failed. Ben & Jerry's presence in Waterbury's Not Quite Independence Day parade and annual pumpkin giveaways assured neighbors that the national brand was still a member of the Waterbury community.

In 2006, Ben & Jerry's added vanilla and chocolate to the ingredients it sourced through fair trade. The company's commitment to fair trade was a clear example of how it used its spending power to express its values. Fair trade certification guaranteed a fair price for farmers who grew the vanilla, cocoa and coffee beans in flavors like Coffee, Coffee BuzzBuzzBuzz! The fair price enabled the farmers to reinvest in their land and communities.

Ben & Jerry's employees were back in the nation's capital in 2007, this time dressed as cloned cows. The U.S. Food and Drug Administration had ruled meat and milk from cloned cows was safe to eat, so employees staged a "Truth or Clone-sequences" protest. A few years later, the protest was in New York, and the cause was Occupy Wall Street. Ben, Jerry and employees supported a rally against increased economic inequality by scooping ice cream in Zuccotti Park.

By the end of the aughts, Ben & Jerry's bona fides as an activist company were well established. Ben Cohen had always said business was the greatest force for social change—it had the power and the responsibility to fight for social and environmental justice. The causes and movements that the company supported fell into these two broad areas, especially when they intersected. Climate change, for example, was a focus because it affects the world's most marginalized people in the most dramatic way.

In 2009, Vermont's civil unions officially became recognized as same-sex marriage. Ben & Jerry's had been providing benefits to domestic partners, regardless of gender, since 1989, so the company was ahead of the curve in embracing marriage equality. To celebrate the home state victory, Chubby Hubby was temporarily renamed Hubby Hubby. Similarly, Oh My! Apple Pie became Apple-y Ever After to support gay marriage in the United Kingdom, and Chocolate Chip Cookie Dough became I Dough, I Dough when same-sex marriage became legal nationwide in the United States. Later, Scoop Shops in Australia would get a lot of media attention for refusing to serve two scoops of the same flavor until marriage equality was passed by parliament. Love is love, the company asserted.

Wordplay, puns and double entendre continued to be an effective way to get consumer attention—especially when paired with memorable flavors—but they weren't without risk. In 2011, Schweddy Balls made a controversial debut with a direct reference to a bawdy *Saturday Night Live* sketch starring Alec Baldwin. The next year, Taste the Lin-Sanity was created by one Scoop Shop in Boston to honor hometown NBA star Jeremy Lin. The flavor had fortune cookie chunks and was accused of being racist. The company apologized.

More successful was Ben & Jerry's venture into non-dairy flavors. A 2014 petition on Change.org drew thousands of signatures from people who craved a non-dairy alternative—one that tasted just as good as ice cream. A commitment to non-dairy, they said, would show the company's commitment to limiting its carbon footprint and fighting climate change. They also felt a Ben & Jerry's offering would go a long way in taking non-dairy mainstream.

The company started with four flavors in 2016 (Chunky Monkey, Chocolate Fudge Brownie, Coffee Caramel Fudge and P.B. & Cookies), choosing an almond base as the blankest "canvas" for the funky, chunky flavors. By 2020, the non-dairy, vegan lineup included fourteen flavors, with promises of more to come.

On a hot day in the summer of 2017, the Waterbury plant was the setting for a protest organized by Migrant Justice. Dairy farm workers marched the thirteen miles between Montpelier and Waterbury, chanting and calling for "Milk with Dignity." On October 3, Ben & Jerry's CEO Jostein Solheim signed an historic agreement with Migrant Justice to implement a worker-led program to protect human rights and labor standards on dairy farms. The signing ended two years of intense negotiations.

By the end of the decade, Ben & Jerry's social activism had zeroed in on racial justice. In the wake of yet another police shooting of a Black man, the company said Black Lives Matter, and the simple statement drew considerable backlash. Undeterred, Ben & Jerry's focused on criminal justice reform and on addressing the broader issue of systemic racism. Art exhibits commemorating the Poor People's Campaign and John Lewis's march across the Edmund Pettus Bridge sprang up at the Waterbury plant's public patio. Justice ReMix'd was launched to support the Advancement Project National Office and grassroots organizations on the ground. When George Floyd was murdered, Ben & Jerry's pulled no punches and said, "We must dismantle white supremacy."

It was 2020. The COVID pandemic upended social norms and spread fear as well as disease. Protests over racial and economic inequality erupted while the country prepared for a divisive presidential election. Ben & Jerry's Scoop Shops and Waterbury's factory tour closed alongside other nonessential businesses, and each day seemed to melt into the next.

With an increased appetite for comfort food, Americans turned to familiar favorites. Scoop Shop sales were down, but pints flew off the freezer shelves at supermarkets. Waterbury factory workers made ice cream 24/7 to keep up with unprecedented demand, despite the extra burden of social distancing, protective equipment and increased sanitation. It was a heroic effort and not out of character for the hardworking men and women on the lines of the Waterbury factory.

So, what happens now? The worldwide impact of COVID and the social disruption that followed in its wake made 2020 a year that many were happy to see end. What *is* known is that there will always be challenges to face and injustice to address. Ben & Jerry's will continue to churn out euphoric flavors and will continue to use the power of its business voice, resources and expertise to fight for its progressive values. As the company grows, its influence and ability to create positive change grow as well.

3

FARM TO TABLE

Laura Kloeti

Waterbury is filled with neighbors who have lived the "movement" before it was in style and is home to a number of the top tourist attractions in the state. Grenier's Farm Stand sold fruits and veggies, pickles and baked goods from 1988 to 2018. Evergreen Gardens of Vermont has grown too many veggies, flowers, plants and herbs to count. The Painted Tulip grows flowers and sells fresh eggs. Then there's Green Mountain Garlic Farm, Moonlight Farm organic produce, Hungry Mountain Orchard, Waterbury Farmers Market, Sunflower Natural Foods and Ben & Jerry's Factory Tour, the number one attraction in the state, whose business practices respect the earth and environment, often infusing their ice cream names with social justice issues. We can't forget Smugglers' Notch Distillery Barrel House Tasting Room and Lake Champlain Chocolates, a Certified B Corporation, committed to "progressive social and environmental business practices, accountability, and transparency." They combine local ingredients with fair trade chocolate. Cold Hollow Cider Mill was purchased in 2000 by Paul and Gayle Brown. Today, they have expanded to include a luncheonette and tasting room, a hard cider line, a jelly room, two cider pressing rooms and a bottling facility. Their Donut Robot produces "one of the four best cider donuts in the country," according to *Gourmet Magazine*, and it is the official donut of the Boston Red Sox. The Browns have a "Honey Bee Corner," bakery, mail order and hundreds of Vermont products available for purchase.

In 2005, Eric Warnstedt opened his celebrated farm-to-table restaurant Hen of the Wood in the location that previously housed a historic gristmill on Stowe Street. He now has three restaurants. Eric was instrumental in making farm to table cool. In 2001, Vermont Artisan Coffee & Tea opened its doors in Mooretown as a manufacturing facility, and then expanded with a café and coffee lab onto Route 100 in Waterbury Center in 2017. Again, sustainability is top priority.

Green Mountain Coffee Roasters (Keurig Green Mountain in 2014–2018, Keurig Dr Pepper 2018–), a leader in environmentalism, follows six practices that the company calls "Brewing a Better World: supply chain communities, supporting local communities, protecting the environment, building demand for sustainable products, working together for change, and creating a great place to work." GMCR has employed thousands of Vermonters. Sadly, by 2018 they had mostly moved out of Waterbury, and the Green Mountain Coffee Roasters Café and Visitor Center closed for good in 2020 during the COVID-19 pandemic.

The Blue Stone features some of Vermont's best pizza and proudly serves as many locally and regionally grown products as possible; it has a full pub menu, an extensive bar and forty-five beer options. Tanglewoods Restaurant, on Guptil Road, served for twenty-five successful years, closing in 2014. It reopened as ZenBarn with the "mission to build our community from soil to soul," offering a globally inspired farm-to-table menu, entertainment, a bar, wellness classes and a mission of environmentally and socially responsible business practices.

The Vermont Fresh Network, established in 1996, was instrumental in linking farmers, chefs and consumers together, and educating, marketing and assisting. Soon more and more people started to see the value of buying local, even making it a mission, and by 2016 lots of restaurants were using at least a few local ingredients.

Packaging is now more eco-friendly, and everyone must compost. In 2000, I recall most takeout containers being made of Styrofoam. Ethnic foods are more popular now, and patrons are more educated and interested in food, where it comes from, cooking and health. This has also resulted in more restaurant special orders. Practices are constantly becoming more sustainable, progressive, socially responsible and innovative. New businesses clearly seem to have the mission in mind and think outside the box.

Through education and understanding we can do more to help ourselves, the farms and the Earth. Kids are our future. Years ago, Chef Michael, of Michael's on the Hill, would go to the elementary schools to teach about eating from the garden. Some kids didn't know what a chive was and had never eaten a raw carrot. Now, the Harwood Union schools have an entire Farm to School Program, including a Jr. Iron Chef competition that "challenges teams of middle and high school students to create healthy, local dishes that inspire school meal programs." Exposure is key.

Our community has been held together by quite a lot—not just talented, driven people. We have overcome everything from the horrendous flood left by Tropical Storm Irene in 2011 in which Main Street and its inhabitants were devastated to the COVID-19 pandemic. We are strong and fierce, and when a friend is in need, help is there. We have all played a role in the good and bad times, giving a hug, preparing a meal, giving what you can or just giving a wave. That is Waterbury, Vermont, and I'm proud to be part of it.

As a result of more product requests, there is now more local, organic availability. Farmers now grow lost ancient heirloom varieties of vegetables. There is true passion between chef, consumer and farmer. Vermont is at the forefront of the farm-to-table movement, with Vermonters rated time and time again as the strongest producers and consumers of local food in the country. There are many talented chefs and producers in Vermont doing their part to promote healthy, local eating.

4

HISTORY OF CIVIL UNIONS AND THE IMPACT ON THE WATERBURY AREA

Willie Docto

The early 2000s was a historic time for tourism in Vermont, specifically for LGBT tourism. In 1999, the Vermont Supreme Court ruled that same-sex couples were entitled to the same legal benefits and responsibilities of any married couple, but it gave the legislature the task of making that happen. The Vermont legislature and Governor Howard Dean passed the first civil union law in the country, a controversial and progressive move. This gave businesses the opportunity to tap into a market that had generally been ignored. On July 1, 2000, the civil union law went into effect and immediately attracted hundreds of couples from around the country to Vermont.

Two inns benefited from this phenomenal opportunity: Moose Meadow Lodge (owned by me and Greg Trulson) and the Grunberg Haus (owned by Jeff and Linda Connor). Between our two inns, we attracted about forty to seventy same-sex weddings a year. Many of them included only the couple, some had a few guests and a few other weddings had over one hundred guests. These weddings helped not only the inns and B&Bs but also restaurants, shops, florists, photographers, planners and others in the wedding industry. I estimated that for each person here for a wedding, the economic impact to the local businesses was about $500. Until Massachusetts and Canada legalized gay marriage in 2004, Vermont had the corner on the gay wedding market.

Gary and Dan's wedding was the first in the country after the repeal of Don't Ask, Don't Tell (DATA). The jubilant officiant (*center*) is Greg Trulson. *Courtesy of Toby Talbot.*

On the state level, there was no special effort to maximize the undeniable economic impact of the civil union law. So, when Governor Jim Douglas came into office, I met with Commissioner of Tourism and Marketing Bruce Hyde (a fellow innkeeper himself in Waitsfield) to strongly urge his office to reach out to the LGBT traveler market. His response was basically that the governor wants to attract all kinds of couples to get married in Vermont. It was not a surprising response but nevertheless a disappointing one.

Several members of the Waterbury Tourism Council supported my efforts, while some were skeptical, and a few were outright against them. It was all new territory for our community, for Vermont and for the country.

I personally saw civil unions not as a political issue but as an economic one. It was good for my business, and it was good for many other businesses in the community. That is why I continued to pursue efforts to target the LGBT traveler market by gathering other likeminded business owners around Waterbury and the state. With them, I founded the Vermont Gay Tourism Association, which, for twenty years, was the only statewide tourism organization in the country whose mission was to market the state as a friendly and welcoming destination for LGBT travelers.

5

MICHAEL'S ON THE HILL

Laura Kloeti

Michael's on the Hill, on Route 100, was the former location of Villa Tragara, the storied Italian restaurant that offered homemade, traditional fare and dinner theater in the barn for over twenty years. To the heartbreak of the community, Tony and Tish DiRuocco closed their doors in 2001. We were welcomed with open arms, as patrons were familiar with driving up the driveway to the beautiful restaurant and vista.

Michael and I met while we worked together in the same restaurant kitchen in his homeland of Switzerland. There, eating from local farms, bartering with artisan-producing neighbors and gardening was the norm. This not only creates a close community but also provides the healthiest, freshest product and supports the local economy. After working for years in some of the finest restaurants in New York, Hawaii and Switzerland, we felt that Vermont's likeminded belief system and small-town values offered the opportunity to nurture relationships with our food producers on an intimate level and provide our young family with what we craved. In 2000, we left Michael's post as chef de cuisine of the St. Regis Hotel in Manhattan for Vermont. It was the best thing we ever did.

Michael's cooking inspiration stems from his childhood—European comfort food, sustainable and unprocessed. By combining his classic training with Vermont's culinary bounty, Michael created his own notable cooking style. In 2002, we found our perfect spot and opened Michael's on the Hill in Waterbury Center in a beautiful circa 1820 farmhouse set on a hill with captivating views of the Green Mountains and sunsets, four acres of land with gardens and forest and an original barn that had been attached to the building with a crane thirty years prior. Our dream has always been to offer locals and tourists alike an "ultimate Vermont dining experience" in a relaxed, welcoming atmosphere. Michael and I have found that the best way to achieve this is by reading what people want and progressing along with them through the changing of the times, through modification of our menus, service and décor.

Michael has done his best to promote and educate throughout our state and country through cooking classes, demonstrations, mentoring and various venues, and on a global level he served as a committee member during the collaboration of the original White Paper on Sustainable Gastronomy for France. He continues to contribute to the paper as it advances each year. He has been a featured chef in various arenas and has been invited as a guest chef to locations spanning from a five-year stint with Disney World's International Food & Wine Festival to Holland America Line Culinary Cruises in locations such as the Caribbean, Australia and Indonesia. Since opening, we have received many accolades, but being Vermont's first Chef of the Year by the Vermont Chamber of Commerce and the First Green Restaurant in the Green Mountain State by the Vermont Department of Agriculture exceed all else because they acknowledge that we have been on the right track with our community.

During this evolution, we have built strong bonds with our staff, producer partners and community. We now have at least thirty local producers on our menu at any given time, and we are certainly not alone.

6

THE OLD STAGECOACH INN

John Barwick

The Stagecoach Inn has had a long and varied history; it was built in 1826 as a stagecoach stop and respite for travelers. It then became a family residence for several generations, following which it returned to its position as a lodging establishment while falling on hard times. The Stagecoach eventually slipped into such disrepair that many wondered what would become of the actual structure.

In 1985, Kim Dow, who was from Waterbury, and her husband, Jim Marcotte, bought the inn and set about bringing it back to life with the help of the Waterbury Historical Society and a substantial loan from the Small Business Administration (SBA). In 1987, after two years of renovation, the inn was transformed into a fully operational bed-and-breakfast with a commercial kitchen supporting a fifty-seat restaurant.

Unfortunately, this endeavor was not met with success. The country was going through a recession, and with interest rates at 15 percent, these combined factors forced the inn to close after a few years in business. The ownership reverted to the SBA, which immediately put it up for sale.

It sat empty for a few years until Jack and John Barwick bought the inn on September 2, 1993. A father-and-son team from Connecticut, they had recently been living in southern Vermont. They were interested in becoming innkeepers and had searched for a property for about a year before deciding on the Old Stagecoach Inn.

Summer photo of the Old Stagecoach Inn located on North Main Street in downtown Waterbury. *Courtesy of H Glenn.*

During the first seven years of their ownership, food service was limited to breakfast and a few private functions and small weddings. There was also a very cozy library bar. In 1997, it was decided to open the restaurant for dinner to both guests and to the public. John and next-door neighbor Nik Armetsaff were hosts and chefs. The menu was largely slow-cooked barbecue with daily specials. To accomplish this, a huge half-ton cast-iron smoker was installed on the back porch and is there to this day. The offering was well received, but the seasonal ebb and flow of the business was difficult to manage. Waterbury was not yet the local food and craft beer destination it is today.

The summer was one of the busiest times, and to increase dining capacity as well as add to the ambience of the inn, a large deck was added to the front of the carriage house in 1999. The umbrella tables added another twenty restaurant seats to the seating for twenty-four in the dining room. This really allowed the busy times to be quite busy. Due to unexpected changes in staff, the restaurant closed, but weddings and private functions were still ongoing, and the inn served a lovely breakfast to guests and locals.

Early in this decade, it was decided the one-hundred-foot pine tree in front of the inn had to be removed for safety reasons. Per Jack's instructions, the tree's trunk was taken to Marshall's chainsaw carving on Route 100. Max Osrio carved a beautiful twelve-foot eagle that was installed on the old tree stump so it could look out over Main Street. It is there to this day.

The inn continued to become more popular, and by 2011, it had achieved respectable occupancy numbers. It was the end of August 2011 when Tropical Storm Irene arrived. The inn was full that night, and a mild, warm rain was falling with a light wind. All seemed calm; drinks were being served on the deck. Around 8:30 p.m., there was a big bang, and the lights went out. Candles and lanterns were distributed to the guests, and complimentary glasses of champagne were offered. If we had only realized that the loud noise we heard was the power substation situated on the Winooski River a quarter mile away—it was actually going under water. Thinking all was calm, we went to bed only to be awakened around 2:30 a.m. to a general alarm klaxon. By that time, the driveway was flooded with three to four feet of water; water was approaching the inn's front door as water was across Main Street. The guests were then evacuated to higher ground, near the nearby church.

The next morning brought an unwelcome sight. Water surrounded the inn. There were twenty cars in the parking lot, with water literally up to the steering wheels. All vehicles would later be determined to be total losses. The water did rise a little higher but still never breached the first floor, which was somewhat of a blessing.

The inn was inoperable and closed for repair. All the inn's essentials and mechanics resided in the basement: boilers, electric, phone, internet, hot water, refrigeration and storage. And all of this was either damaged or destroyed. Efforts to open the inn depended on first pumping out the basements, then mucking out the mud and debris, next determining what could be salvaged and what needed to be replaced. Truck-size dumpsters were filled with ruined goods and hauled away. Days later, the basements were pumped out and drying; the electricity, phone and internet services were restored; and amazingly the inn reopened in a limited fashion ten days later.

Over the next five to six years the inn continued to increase in popularity, and throughout the year, except for the slow seasons before summer and before winter, it was bustling.

Jack had always been an integral part of the inn's operations, greeting guests, taking reservations, cooking for special parties and even bartending. It was amazing how much he contributed late into his eighties. He could often be found in an armchair in front of the fire in the parlor entertaining guests with tales of the past. He had many rich and varied life experiences before he arrived at the inn, so tall tales were not in short supply.

As the years went on, medical issues, as well as old age, caught up with him. Fortunately, the inn was a perfect place for him in his later years. He could do as much or as little as he wanted because John and the staff were always available if he needed help. The fact that there were always things to do and people to engage with kept him sharp, and his mental acuity was formidable.

Jack passed away in August 2018 at ninety-two years of age. Two weeks prior he was presiding over a family reunion and was in good spirits. Those who knew him agreed it was a life well lived.

The weekend of Jack's memorial was the only time the inn was voluntarily closed in all its years. But the inn was fully booked for the rest of the summer and coming foliage season, so life continued.

One guiding principle for John was that the inn would remain in the family as long as Jack was alive, as it was Jack's home and an excellent alternative to assisted living or a nursing home. With Jack gone, John considered his options. Although John loved the inn, its surroundings and Vermont, for the last twenty-seven years, any serious travel had not been possible. He very much desired to see more of the world. With much ambivalence, John decided to put the inn on the market.

The years leading up to 2020 continued the upward occupancy until the abrupt interruption of the COVID-19 pandemic. As the pandemic worsened, the order eventually came from the governor in March to close all lodging establishments. The inn was able to reopen three months later on June 15, but only to Vermont residents. As the pandemic seemed to abate, restrictions were loosened, and the inn could accommodate interstate travelers with mandated precautions. This was the same for bars and restaurants. Vermont had been a leader in the country with low COVID numbers, which was attributed to the state's strict travel guidelines. However, following foliage season, infection rates across the country spiked, so tighter travel restrictions were imposed, again bringing interstate travel to a trickle. This is our current situation; however, with available grants and loans, the inn continues to survive. It is thought that once travel opens again there will be a flood of the inn's longtime guests eager to return.

With the pandemic's arrival, there has been little interest from potential buyers; however, it is still on the market. Time will tell. It is hoped that the Stagecoach Inn will remain much as it is now, an old-fashioned, lodging-based establishment welcoming travelers from near and far with a dose of warm and personal Vermont hospitality.

7

VERMONT ARTISAN COFFEE & TEA CO. AND COFFEE LAB INTERNATIONAL

Holly Alves

It was bright and early Monday morning, August 29, 2011, when Matt Hunt arrived at Coffee Lab International for his first day of work. A recent graduate of Elon University in North Carolina, Matt was excited to return home to Vermont and begin work as a laboratory assistant, learning all about the specialty coffee industry from the owner and renowned coffee cupper Mané Alves. With this he would begin testing coffees for companies such as Dunkin' Donuts, IHOP and Green Mountain Coffee Roasters. Mané, a longtime Waterbury Center resident and "coffeepreneur," had started Coffee Lab International fifteen years earlier and was renting a five-thousand-square-foot facility at 80 Commercial Plaza in Moretown. Sure enough, when Mané met Matt outside the front door that morning, instead of a broad, welcoming smile, Mané had a look on his face of shock and disbelief.

The night before, Tropical Storm Irene had come barreling through town, flooding everything in its wake, Mané's businesses included. Four and a half feet of the Winooski River had inundated not only Coffee Lab but also its sister company and specialty coffee roastery Vermont Artisan Coffee & Tea. Bags and bags of green coffee were ruined. The expensive sixty-kilo Renegade Roaster had been sitting in water for hours as well as the tea-making machine. Mud and muck were everywhere. It was devastating.

Thankfully, repairs to the building were made, the equipment bounced back and the employees hung in there working through mold remediation

Holly Alves and Mané Alves of Vermont Artisan Coffee and Tea Company are featured in the coffee lab. *Courtesy of Brent Harrewyn.*

and months of construction. The community support was heartwarming. Still, Mané vowed never to go through that kind of disaster again and was determined to find a new site. His vision included offering a world-class facility for coffee analysis, evaluation and roasting, as well as a coffee school. He wanted the new facility to be visible to locals and tourists alike. He wanted to own the land and the building. And he didn't want it sitting in a floodplain.

Fast-forward six years. Now if you are driving along Route 100 between Waterbury and Stowe, you can't miss the big red barn with its silver silo that says *Coffee* in bold letters. This is certainly by no means out of place for a community like ours whose residents are used to the iconic look of barns as well as the familiar aroma of roasted coffee. With the indelible mark and success that Green Mountain Coffee Roasters (now Keurig Dr Pepper) has left on the town, being the "other coffee company" has enabled the business to somewhat fly under the radar. That is, until now.

Mané swung open the doors to the new fifteen-thousand-square-foot facility at the end of 2017. He oversaw the design and construction of the custom-built barn, working closely with local architect Joe Greene and builder John Connor, owner of Connor Construction out of Montpelier. Mané also worked with local solar company SunCommon to create a twenty-space solar carport on site. The energy-efficient building is heated by wood pellet burners instead of fossil fuels and houses the three prior coffee businesses and one new one: Coffee Lab International, CLI's School of Coffee, Vermont Artisan Coffee & Tea Co. and a new café.

With the additional square footage, Coffee Lab has spread out with a dry lab on one side of the building and a wet lab on the other. There is also a dedicated classroom for CLI's School of Coffee. Students come from all over the country and the world to take various coffee courses, where they learn how to cup coffee and become official "Q Graders." The School of Coffee also offers hands-on roasting classes and barista classes. As one of the finer specialty coffee production and education facilities in all New England, if not the country, CLI's classroom has been designated and certified as one of the Specialty Coffee Association of America's premier campus destinations.

The majority of the facility's square footage is taken up by Vermont Artisan Coffee & Tea Roastery. There are three large, forty-foot-high indoor grain silos that hold green coffee. On the production floor is a range of roasters for both production and training purposes, including a three-kilo Diedrich that roasts sample coffee kits for Q Instructors, a 5-kilo Probat, a 15-kilo Giesen, a wood-fired 15-kilo Ghibli roaster, a 60-kilo machine from Renegade Roaster Design Group and a new 90-kilo Ghibli. Looking around stacked on pallets you notice 130-pound burlap bags stamped with exotic coffee origins: Burundi, for example, Café de Monteverde, Costa Rica, Honduras Arabica Washed and Mugaga AB, Produce of Kenya.

Tucked in the far back of the production floor is a room dedicated entirely to tea. Whole leaf premium teas are stored in coolers. When opened, their distinctive aromas waft through the room. The peppermint will make your eyes water, the ginger lemongrass will make you pucker and the Earl Grey is scented with bergamot blossoms. The room houses the tea machine, which forms the teas into triangular sachets, made from 100 percent biodegradable mesh material.

The newest addition to the coffee venture is Vermont Artisan's Coffee Bar and Café located on the south side of the building. "The fact we are so visible from the road brought in many customers who were maybe not familiar with our coffee before. The Café is now the best way for folks to sample our various coffees and learn all about them from our Baristas," Mané Alves recently told *Daily Coffee News*. "The customers then tend to travel home and order the coffees and teas online. Our bright red coffee barn and the different businesses in it are giving us a level of visibility and of authenticity we just hadn't had before," commented Alves. "Plus, we have many locals who stop by to see how we became a coffee café. Our staff tends to know them not only by name but by their favorite beverage of choice," he added.

Many customers who visit wonder about Mane's background; where he is from, and what brought him here to Waterbury, Vermont? A native of Lisbon, Portugal, Mané was working in quality control and as a winemaker during the mid-eighties in the Alexander Valley of Northern California. It was during that time in the late eighties, while on a ski trip to Squaw Valley, he happened to hop on a quad chairlift as the "single." That's when he met his future wife, Holly. They had known each other for three weeks when Holly, a marketing executive living in San Francisco and working for the lifestyle company Esprit, was recruited to be the head of marketing for Ben & Jerry's. The couple moved from California to Waterbury Center in 1990, and Mané translated his winemaking and tasting skills to the coffee industry. That eventually led to the creation of the Coffee Lab, and in 2001 came Vermont Artisan Coffee & Tea.

Holly has been active in the business since 2011. She was instrumental in securing a bridge loan from the Vermont Economic Development Authority (VEDA) after Tropical Storm Irene hit. She has also built relationships with lenders and banks such as Northfield Savings for the construction monies. Mané often travels all over the world, visiting coffee farms on three continents as well as fulfilling coffee and teaching contracts in Japan, China and Taiwan. Holly handles all the marketing and branding efforts for the companies as well as directing the day-to-day businesses in Mané's absence.

People in the coffee community and elsewhere have come to think of Waterbury as "The Coffee Town." This mostly stems from Green Mountain Coffee Roasters' longtime presence here and the company's remarkable and unparalleled success. Now, as it has become Keurig Dr Pepper and moved on to greener pastures, so to speak, Mané hopes to keep the specialty coffee mantle here and continue the tradition of handcrafting delicious coffees. "I have no intention of being bought out by the Nestlés and Unilevers of the world," Mané recently commented. "I love what I do. Holly and I are so grateful for our employees and for the support of the entire community. We're here for the long haul. Not even another one-hundred-year flood will get me to move again."

8

WATERBURY BRAND HISTORY

Jeanne Kirby

At a July 2008 Vermont Downtown Program retreat, then Revitalizing Waterbury executive director Jeanne Kirby was introduced to Tripp Muldrow, an accomplished urban planner and partner of the Greenville, South Carolina–based firm Arnett Muldrow. That meeting planted the first seed of a multiyear, productive collaboration.

Between 2008 and early 2011, steps were taken by RW to prioritize programmatic work that would lead to specific strategies to develop a comprehensive Waterbury marketing and branding plan. In the spring of 2011, RW hosted its first public forum on the general subject of community image building, presented by Tripp Muldrow. During that same trip to Vermont, Tripp was given an extensive nooks-and-crannies tour of Waterbury Village and Waterbury Center conducted by RW board member Jack Carter and Executive Director Jeanne Kirby. That outing, in hindsight, was kismet, as it was a pre-Irene version of our community life, economy and infrastructure.

The Waterbury Brand came to be with the involvement of the community's input and was encouraged and supported by Revitalizing Waterbury.

A couple months after Tropical Storm Irene, RW hosted a November 2011 Vermont Downtown Program Networking meeting at the American

Legion. This gathering was an opportunity to inspire and share with downtown managers from around the state Waterbury's post–tropical storm recovery progress to date. In addition, guest speakers Tripp Muldrow and Todd Barnum from the National Main Street Program further educated key Waterbury stakeholders about the why and the how of community branding.

As part of the FEMA Long Term Community Recovery (LTCR) process in 2012, RW became the sponsor of the Community Image Building/ Market Retail Study. This was one of several projects supported by the community. In July, Green Mountain Coffee Roasters awarded a $10,000 grant to RW; this funded a market assessment workshop in September 2012, led by Tripp Muldrow. For three days, four roundtable and focus groups met, with eight one-on-one interviews conducted. Additionally, nearly forty Waterbury businesses participated in a targeted survey. The following month, preliminary market study findings were presented to all business participants; they also received an individual business report that provided details about their customer base in comparison to other Waterbury businesses.

RW secured an additional $5,000 in grant funding from Northfield Savings Bank, Ben and Jerry's Community Action Team and the Waterbury Tourism Council to conduct Phase 2 of this project, which was a three-day community image-building workshop in mid-January 2013. That effort culminated in a public brand reveal event that garnered feedback from the standing-room-only crowd. The purpose of the branding and marketing strategy was to better position Waterbury to capture market opportunities, solidify community pride, aspire to future goals and provide a unified approach for Waterbury to better relate its brand story. This was well received, with some parts of the branding package not accepted. Further refinements to the brand identity were made, and the Waterbury Select Board provided $5,000 for implementation. The final Community Brand Identity Guidelines were made accessible by RW to the town, community organizations and businesses as a resource. These guidelines encouraged more effective and cohesive community promotion to residents, investors and visitors. The brand is actively used within the community for events, community promotion and digital formats.

9

WHY CRAFT BEER? WHY WATERBURY?

Liz Schlegel

As the editors were putting this book together, they realized that there should be a section about beer, since it has been such a huge part of Waterbury's revitalization. As it says on the Blackback Pub's website, "At The Blackback we are all about the beer. It is the reason we are here. We proudly cater to the many beer fans from all over the world. Waterbury, Vermont is the Epicenter of beer in the Northeast and arguably one of the finest in the nation. We also recognize the important role beer has played in this town's recent history. From beer comes life and vitality, which is reflected in our locavore farm-to-plate business model." Many, many residents and visitors to Waterbury would passionately agree.

In the beginning, there was craft food. There was a positive and creative food synergy happening in Waterbury, building from the long roots of Ben & Jerry's and Green Mountain Coffee Roasters and the many small food entrepreneurs who got their start here. Locals and visitors alike were starting to appreciate Waterbury as a place where excellent food was made and could be found—*New York Times* food writer Mark Bittman was an early and passionate fan, putting the area on the map for traveling foodies. In 1998, in a two-hundred-year-old former gristmill, renowned food experts Robin Schempp and Steve Schimoler founded one of Vermont's finest locavore restaurants, the Mist Grill. The white-tablecloth restaurant put Waterbury on the map for dedicated food lovers in Vermont and across the Northeast.

Just a short way from the acclaimed Mist Grill was the local favorite Arvad's. The friendly neighborhood pub and grill was founded in 1989 by Jeffrey and MaryAnne Larkin, who prided themselves on serving more than one hundred beers from around the world. There were other restaurants in town, but Arvad's was the first to focus on showcasing a wide variety of beers and tempting the beer aficionado with unique imports as well as Vermont-made beers from upstart breweries like Middlebury's Otter Creek and Long Trail Ale from Bridgewater Corners.

In 2003, John and Jen Kimmich came to town and started The Alchemist on the corner of Main and Elm Streets, down the street from Arvad's. They knew they wanted to open a brewpub in Vermont, and they chose Waterbury because it was a great location within a stone's throw of Stowe, Burlington, Montpelier and several ski areas, with a strong foodie culture already. Jen noted, "The success of the [Mist Grill] signaled to us that Waterbury was indeed a good fit and being overlooked." From the outset, they were brewing beers of unusual quality, and they soon built up a cult following. Locals enjoyed the casual atmosphere, welcoming staff and the delicious and affordable food and beer; the ski crowd obsessed over the delicious fries and the famous Heady Topper double IPA. By the mid-2000s, there was always a long line, and that had its effects on other local entrepreneurs.

The elegant James Beard Award–winning restaurant Hen of the Wood opened in the Mist Grill space in Waterbury in 2005. Hen of the Wood cofounder Eric Warnstedt recalled, "Hen was here just before the [craft beer] boom so it didn't influence us moving here but…the craft beer scene has deep roots in Vermont. Waterbury got its time in the spotlight with the original Alchemist brewpub. I can remember the first keg of Heady Topper being tapped and the collins-type glass John Kimmich liked the beer served in. Special times indeed!"

Mark Frier, who founded The Reservoir in 2008—originally Waterbury Wings, just a few steps away from Arvad's and The Alchemist, at the top of Bank Hill—has his own story of the impact of Waterbury's craft beer scene on his life.

> *Beer weirdly and luckily moved me to Waterbury. I was in my twenties, moving to Vermont from Chicago in 2006, and as soon as I stepped into the Alchemist, and tried their beer, I wanted to move to town. I did about a month later. I enjoyed the beer at the pub and ate there three to four days a week. My little neighborhood pub quickly grew so busy, I found*

it increasingly difficult to go to because of its popularity. I saw the influx of out-of-state plates and saw what beer could do for tourism in the state.

A year or two later, I attended the Vermont Brewers Festival on the Waterfront in Burlington and wondered why restaurants, at the time, did not have draft lists that represented all the Vermont microbreweries I saw. Usually just a few here or a few there. After trying to go to The Alchemist on a Tuesday and being told it was a two-hour wait, the idea of The Reservoir was born. The idea was to complement the Alchemist and give patrons access to the other beers of the state that we felt were their best at the time along with comfort food using local ingredients when possible. Waterbury Wings gave me a great foundation on which to build, a local's restaurant with a great bar and customer base. The most difficult conversations were with distributors that felt some ownership of the beer list—letting them know we *would direct what beers we wanted on our lines, a concept that seemed simple but at the time was not the trend. Soon after that, Blackback opened with a very similar focus bringing even more beers and options including many from Europe. Beer tourism took off and then you saw additions of retail stores like Craft Beer Cellar.*

Watching The Alchemist go under after Tropical Storm Irene was devastating. It still was my favorite pub and I built a restaurant to complement it in so many ways. I remember helping empty the flooded basement and holding a dripping wet computer and being told the recipes were on that computer, it was a moment I will never forget. Hearing it was not reopening was devastating but I also got to try a Heady Topper in a can for the first time, allowing the brand and the beer to live on. Prohibition Pig went into the former pub space and continued the momentum of incredible beer and craft cocktails, continuing to keep the beer energy in town alive.

Where beer is headed, hard to say, but I think drinking local craft beer will continue for those who live here and those who visit.

Rick Binet opened Waterbury's Blackback Pub and Flyshop in 2009. The tiny hole-in-the-wall opened in a former barbershop and, in its earliest incarnation, had just enough room for a display of fishing equipment, delicious beers, a handful of committed beer enthusiasts and the friendly, chatty Rick. Over time, the space was expanded to fill the original footprint of the long-defunct Waterbury Pub, adding food and table service. Regular patrons Lynn Mason and Dave Juenker bought the pub in 2014 and have presided over this thriving and much-beloved downtown staple since then.

Over the years, the success of The Alchemist had created a nexus of beer-loving pubs and restaurants around Bank Hill in Waterbury. If the Alchemist was too crowded, you could hop across the street to the Blackback, or Arvad's or The Reservoir. Beer lovers had an astonishing array of choices, all downtown and walkable. You could even get great beers at Cork, the wine bar. And the great choices continued to expand.

In 2011, Tropical Storm Irene reshaped the downtown landscape, closing The Alchemist Pub & Brewery. While Alchemist's Waterbury Cannery opened immediately afterward, the loss of the pub left a hole in the downtown landscape. While John and Jen were focusing on growing their beer canning business, they wanted to make sure another restaurant opened in that spot. Thus, Prohibition Pig was born. Original founder Chad Rich brought his love of craft beer, artisanal cocktails and North Carolina barbecue to the popular corner location.

The Blue Stone opened on Stowe Street, around the corner from the Blackback, in late 2012. As owners Vinny Petrarca and Chris Fish say on their website, "The Blue Stone story began with our love of exceptional pizza, rustic simple food and great beer." This welcome addition to the downtown dining and drinking scene provided another key food group—pizza—as well as more of the renowned beers that were drawing more and more folks to Waterbury.

The runaway success of Heady Topper, renowned as one of the world's top beers since its launch, inspired other brewers to try their hands at hazy IPAs and to create and share their own beers in Waterbury. Prohibition Pig began brewing beers in 2013 and opened a full brewery and tasting room next door in 2014. Other flagship Vermont breweries Lawson's Finest Liquids and Hill Farmstead made sure their beers were flowing in Waterbury taps, where the discerning customers could sample several of the world's finest brews back-to-back. In 2014, Hill Farmstead hosted its fourth anniversary party as a pub crawl in downtown Waterbury, and beer lovers stood in long lines to visit each of the selected establishments and try the one-of-a-kind brews provided by Hill Farmstead, Lawson's and the Alchemist to honor the special occasion. It was an all-weekend downtown brewfest, celebrated with joy and camaraderie by beer lovers from across the United States.

Victor Osinaga and Mark Drutman opened Craft Beer Cellar across from Prohibition Pig in late 2013 to support Waterbury's craft beer habit. Their popular store carries nearly one thousand small-batch craft beers. In a 2015 *Seven Days* article, Osinaga said they deliberately chose Waterbury

because they see it as "the epicenter of craft beer in Vermont." Finding and sharing specialty beer offerings from emerging brewers is a natural complement to the many restaurants and pubs that serve the beer lovers.

In 2015, the Ewald family started VERMONT BEER SHEPHERD, based in Duxbury, to bring rare beers to the Vermont market. Their unique distribution model has helped them build beer relationships all over the world, and they have made it possible for Vermonters to get their hands on very special beers.

John Kimmich has long said, if he wanted to brew beer for just himself, he could have been a happy home brewer. But he and Jen wanted more: "We created this atmosphere where people connect, where people are smiling and having fun. That's the whole point of a great beer and a great business—creating that glimmer at the end of the day."

In 2015 and 2016, author James Fallows and his wife, Deb, crisscrossed the country looking for signs of success in small communities. In March 2016, they published their list of "Eleven Signs That a City Will Succeed." Number eleven on the list? The presence of craft breweries. Jim wrote: "A town that has craft breweries also has a certain kind of entrepreneur, and a critical mass of mainly young (except for me) customers." Waterbury has many of the signs on the Fallowses' list, including a downtown, a civic story, creative schools and local patriots. And we have, in abundance, the presence of craft breweries, craft beer and those who love the craft of beer.

PART XIII

TRAGEDIES AND DISASTERS

1

COVID-19 RESPONSE

Barb Farr

In a normal year, the appointed position of emergency management director (EMD) is usually one of working behind the scenes to update the annual Waterbury Emergency Operations Plan and to train, exercise and plan for and respond to any emergencies and/or natural or human-made disasters that may occur. Fortunately, there were no significant natural events causing physical damage to property or persons this past year. Unfortunately, 2020 was the focus of a once-in-a-century worldwide pandemic that has affected our daily lives.

In response to warning signs in early 2020, Waterbury formed a COVID-19 Planning Team in the beginning of March to address potential and unknown effects to our community. This team remains active and is composed of key representatives in our community who are likely to be at the forefront of affected areas. Organizations and groups represented include medical, emergency response, library, schools, Good Neighbor Fund, Waterbury Area Food Shelf, Senior Center/Meals on Wheels, daycares, business concerns, media, business representatives, local officials and town staff.

The purpose for this team is to identify trends, gaps and emergent needs in Waterbury due to the COVID-19 virus and to share resources and information.

All emergency preparedness training that had been scheduled during 2020 was canceled due to the COVID-19 pandemic and resulted in town staff implementing real-life Continuity of Operations procedures. COVID-19

activities include receiving weekly briefings from the State Emergency Operations Center, distributing weekly State Situation Reports to the Waterbury COVID-19 Planning Team, monthly calls, follow-up notes to the team and forwarding Waterbury-area COVID-19 testing site schedules to team members to post on their various websites.

Town manager Bill Shepeluk and library director Almy Landauer quickly instituted a work-from-home policy for municipal and library staff where possible and instituted closure of the municipal offices and library to be consistent with guidelines from the Vermont Department of Health and Governor Scott's emergency orders. Once the initial stay-at-home order became less restrictive, the town offices began providing essential services by appointment. Most public meetings were and still are conducted virtually through Zoom.

The library became the facilitator for Waterbury CARES, a resource for people who would like to volunteer or donate services and those who have unmet needs. In essence, CARES is a matchmaking service, and many matches have been made over the last eleven-plus months. In addition, the library has been able to operate within the changing guidelines by offering virtual programs and providing curbside service for books and library items.

Jon Scott at the Central Vermont Hospital continues to provide insight into the medical adjustments and COVID statistics in our region. Mark Podgewaite, director of Waterbury Ambulance, provides weekly updates on testing services in Waterbury and surrounding towns. Gary Dillon contributes reports on community status and vaccinations for the first responders.

Of highest concern are local seniors, those out of work and anyone in need of assistance. A network of information flows between the schools, Senior Center/Meals on Wheels, the Good Neighbor Fund, the Waterbury Area Food Shelf and the library, as these resources have been invaluable for keeping a pulse on community needs. So far, our community has been fortunate to have avoided being severely overwhelmed through the generosity of those who have helped their friends, families and neighbors in need.

Revitalizing Waterbury has been extremely helpful in sharing grant opportunities, technical assistance and creative marketing to help keep people employed and/or offer temporary solutions to changing needs.

The Town of Duxbury has provided frequent updates as a neighboring community. Our local officials keep tabs on what is going on and provide big-picture guidance. Liz Schlegel, through her facilitation and public service background, ties together the regular Zoom meetings and provides valuable connections with state and federal programs.

Lisa Scagliotti has been proactive in getting important information out to the residents of Waterbury and beyond through the newly formed Waterbury Roundabout, both online and in print, after the *Waterbury Record* stopped printing the weekly newspaper in March 2020.

The COVID-19 Planning Team will continue to meet virtually into 2021 until the coronavirus is under control and it becomes safe to resume normal activities. Although there are approximately thirty-five people representing many organizations that receive Waterbury COVID-19 planning information, the main core of active contributors is listed here.

Sincerely,

Barbara Farr, emergency management director
Mike Bard
Vicki Brooker
Allison Conyers
Gary Dillon
Alyssa Johnson
Dani Kehlmann
Almy Landauer
Karl Lander
Ariel Mondlak
Karen Nevin
Peter Plagge
Mark Podgewaite
Lisa Scagliotti
Liz Schlegel
Jonathan Scott
Bill Shepeluk
Tom Stevens
Theresa Wood
Erik Zetterstrom

2

COVID-19

Youth Perspective

The COVID-19 pandemic has affected every aspect of our community, especially our youth population. The Waterbury Historical Society asked local students to reflect on their experiences since the pandemic began by answering one of the prompts below. We received responses from students of all ages and have picked a small number to represent a variety of experiences.

- What has been the best part and/or worst part of the pandemic?
- Describe how a particular part of your life has been impacted (good or bad) by the pandemic.
- Write a letter to yourself during the pandemic. What do you want your future self to know about this time?
- How will you describe this time to future generations? What important aspects of this experience should be remembered and shared?

Fineas Alfini, Age 5¾

Question: What would you say being in Waterbury was like for you during the last pandemic year?

> *We never go to Waterbury, unless we have to go to Waterbury. We mostly just went through it. We have to wear masks. We go to The Reservoir* [restaurant, for takeout], *or the grocery store. I like masks. I think they are a good idea to keep people safe. The Children's Room is shut down, so we don't go there anymore.*
>
> *Good Parts—Things I learned during the pandemic: winking, snapping, whistling, clicking (tongue), skiing, chairlifting, Star Wars Legos*

Charlotte Burks, Age 12

Letter to Past Self

> *So there's this thing coming. It's called a pandemic, it's what everyone is joking about. You are going to come home from school and get the call that school is going to be closed for a couple of weeks. You'll enjoy being at home and not having to ride the bus over the horrible roads. You will FaceTime your friends every day for many hours. You are going to be stuck at home with your teenage brother and parents. Who are also using the internet for work. After school calls, your parents will tell you about the growing numbers of cases of Coronavirus. It will scare you, but you know you will be okay because you live in Vermont, which is the only safe-ish state.*
>
> *Then you find out that you aren't going back to school for the rest of the year. The ground will be good for planting plants and you will do agility with your dog. Sports will be cancelled and you will start to go insane. Once the weather is warmer your day will be full of bike rides and swimming. You will make a tiny circle of people you hang out and socialize with. Once it is summer you'll go to the Reservoir with your friends and start to think that the numbers are going down, until you hear that they are just getting worse.*
>
> *And that's all I can tell you, I don't want to spoil all the surprises, but you know how you've been talking about a puppy….yeah. Just know you will make it through and your family and friends will stay close. And make it clear that <u>you are not alone</u>.*

Lincoln Gage, Age 13

April 14, 2021

Dear Lincoln,

The Covid-19 pandemic has made 2020–2021 stand out. Wearing masks, obsessively sanitizing and social distancing became a way of life. I have not been able to see friends or extended family for a long time. Activities like eating at restaurants and playing soccer on a team have not occurred. A simple daily task like driving in a car no longer happens.

My parents opted for remote schooling. We took school and our life on the road. Our many adventures have taken us to places like Glacier; Grand Teton, where we saw a grizzly bear, moose, marmots and came within twenty feet of a black bear; Mesa Verde, were we hiked to petroglyphs and saw ruins of old Native American villages; Grand Canyon where we hiked deep into the canyon; Sun Valley with awesome hiking in the Sawtooths; the Dakotas where we visited Mount Rushmore, Crazy Horse and spent time in the Black Hills; Bryce Canyon with its vibrant orange hoodoos; Telluride, where we mountain biked on the elaborate network of trails; Canyonlands; and Arches. It has been truly amazing to explore our beautifully diverse country during this time, something that would never have happened if it were not for Covid.

Poppy, my grandfather, suffered from an ever worsening case of ALS. We drove to Lubec, Maine to spend some quality time and give him one last squeeze. He eventually passed away in December, which has been hard for me to process. Despite the bad things happening in the world during this pandemic, I feel fortunate to have had this unique time with my family and these life changing experiences I will remember for the rest of my life.

Love,
13 (soon to be 14) year old Lincoln
P.S. Also, happy we have a new president.

Zoe LeGeros, Age 10

April, 2021

The best part of the pandemic has been that I have gotten closer to my family because for the first few months of the pandemic we were literally together every single day. We would eat breakfast, lunch, and dinner together. My sister and I also helped my dad with a few podcasts about COVID-19,

and I think that also brought us closer together because we would talk about what it felt like. My sister and I got closer, too. I would help her with her work a lot, and if there was something she thought she could work on more, she would come to me and ask me if I could teach her about it. But those were the good parts.

I think the worst parts were social distancing and online school. I mean, I know that all of those things are helping us, but it's no fun. I haven't been able to hug any of my friends for more than a year. And you would never notice it, but there are a lot of things that you can't do when you are six feet from each other. You can't high five, you can't hug, you can't even touch each other. And online school is super hard. School is not any fun at all when you are staring at a screen all day. You can't do hands-on learning, you can't ask for help as easily, and if both of your parents are in meetings, or just can't help you, what are you supposed to do? Especially if you are in first or second grade, what if you wouldn't know how to do some of your work, and you can't email your teachers? What are you supposed to do? For me, those are the worst, and best parts of the pandemic.

Sincerely,

Zoe LeGeros

Beacan Sadowsky, Age 11

I'm disappointed

I'm disappointed.

I'm disappointed in all the adults who are supposed to be more "mature" than kids. The adults who don't care about anyone but themselves. Who don't care about keeping others safe.

I'm disappointed in all of the people who decided not to wear masks or social distance.

I'm disappointed in myself for not helping enough with the people who need help most.

But most of all I'm disappointed in all of the people who didn't try hard enough. Who made people feel pain because they lost their family and friends. Put yourself in the people's shoes who have lost their friends and family from the pandemic. Feel the pain they feel. Realize that you have been making the wrong choices. Realize that you need to change your actions so you don't hurt any more people by your actions.

But I'm also grateful for all the people who have helped the people in need.

I'm grateful for all the kids who have been more "mature" than adults and speaking up for what they need.

I'm grateful for doctors, who must feel so much pain for not being able to save every person who comes to the hospital with Covid.

Addison Thomas, Age 14

The COVID-19 pandemic has been very challenging for people of all ages. The biggest impact that this pandemic has had on me is my mental health.

Before Covid, the thought of being home and not having to get out of pajamas sounded great; I could sleep in and not have to worry about making sure I had everything together for school the next morning. Now that I am living like this, that idea has become less luxurious. I never would have imagined that drinking enough water and playing with my dog would be a task. Turns out the pandemic affected my mental health more than I anticipated.

My biggest mental health challenge is online learning. When this pandemic shut schools down I, along with thousands and thousands of students and staff members, had to learn how to use technology that none of us knew how to use and we had to adapt to the new circumstances this pandemic brought.

For me the biggest effect of online learning is getting used to working on a screen all day. I find myself feeling more tired throughout the day and am less motivated to do basic everyday tasks that used to come easy. I am having to teach myself how to use technology that I am not used to, how to schedule my day so I can still move around and take care of myself, and even how to educate myself on different subjects. I never realized the value of in-person learning and how being at school helps my overall wellbeing.

Though I have had my share of struggles, I still try to remember the positive outcomes this experience has given me such as learning how to manage my time and assignments.

3
HARWOOD STRONG

David Goodman

On October 8, 2016, five local teenagers were killed in a car crash caused by a wrong-way driver on Interstate 89 between Williston and Richmond. The students were Eli Brookens (Waterbury), Janie Cozzi (Fayston), Liam Hale (Fayston), Mary Harris (Moretown) and Cyrus Zschau (Moretown). Cozzi attended Kimball Union Academy in Meriden, New Hampshire, while the other four students were juniors at Harwood Union High School.

In the days and months that followed, the community came together through a number of events to grieve and heal together. Nearly a year after the crash on October 5, 2017, Harwood Union High School dedicated a gazebo in honor of the five students. David Goodman, chairman of the Harwood Union High School Board, shared the following speech at the dedication.

Grief. Community. Healing. Hope.

Those are like four streams that have been braided together, meandering through our lives this past year.

A day after we learned that we had lost Eli, Mary, Cyrus, Liam and Janie, we acted on instinct: *we came together*. That's what we do in good times, to cheer our teams or give standing O's at our musicals, and in hard times, like this. I remember within hours of the crash last year, hundreds of students

instinctively gathered in school, and later thousands of people gathered on the soccer field to share, hug, cry, and begin our journey of healing.

We called ourselves Harwood Strong. And when we didn't feel very strong, we let others carry us. Our friends. Our families. Our teachers. Our community. Our state. We just knew we had to keep moving forward, with the spirit of our five friends to guide us. We continued the journey…together.

Without realizing it, this small school in the heart of the Green Mountains, showed a whole state how we grieve, how we heal, and how we celebrate life…we do it together.

Celebrating life is what this gazebo is all about. It's a place to hang out, to make music, to laugh and cry, to be together. I can't think of a better way for the Senior Class to honor the spirit of these five amazing friends. I'm pretty sure our 5 stars have already brightened it up with some good laughs there.

Thank you, Harwood students and staff and our five families, for leading us on this journey of healing and hope. You have shown us all the true meaning of what it means to be Harwood Strong.

4

REBUILD WATERBURY

Recovery from Tropical Storm Irene

Theresa A.M. Wood

On August 28, 2011, Tropical Storm Irene, 290 miles wide, swept up the East Coast and across Vermont, dropping up to eleven inches of water from Brattleboro to Bolton. At least forty-five towns were severely hit, including Waterbury—18 homes were lost and another 202 sustained considerable damage. More than 440 claims were made to the Federal Emergency Management Agency (FEMA) from the 05676 zip code, totaling in excess of $2.6 million to homeowners.

Municipal leaders quickly realized that residents would need assistance to recover from the devastation and to organize fundraising. They reached out to Revitalizing Waterbury (the town's state-designated downtown organization that ordinarily assisted businesses) to develop a plan. The RW board of directors quickly stepped up to engage community volunteers to form a special project team that became known as ReBuild Waterbury (RBW). A group of community volunteers formed a steering committee[1] to guide recovery efforts for eligible households covered by the 05676 zip code, so it included parts of Duxbury and Bolton as well. RBW became designated as Waterbury's long-term recovery group. Waterbury was one of the first towns to mobilize such a group and was the first to complete its recovery work and shut down after helping 105 families in their recovery journey in a seventeen-month period.

1. The ReBuild Waterbury Steering Committee members were Mica Cassara, Alison Friedkin, Rob Hofmann, Bob McNamara, MK Monley, Chris Nordle (vice-chair), Dave Rapaport, Lisa Scagliotti and Theresa Wood (chair).

ReBuild Waterbury began to raise funds that would be needed to help community members. Many individual and organization grants and donations were received in excess of $1 million, including resources from the Vermont Disaster Relief Fund. In order to effectively complete the work that needed to be done, RBW made the decision to employ three staff: construction manager Dave Kerr, volunteer coordinator/case manager Mame McKee and project manager/case manager Theresa Wood. There were many households in need—thousands of questions to answer; thousands of volunteer labor hours to be found and organized; dozens of construction projects to be evaluated, prioritized, staged and completed—*all simultaneously*! RBW actively worked with ReTrain/Youth Build, a project of ReSource. They provided many hours of labor and in turn learned valuable skills while on the job. Other organizations that provided countless hours of volunteer labor included the Waterbury Rotary Club, Green Mountain Coffee Roasters, Habitat for Humanity (Williston office) and Vermont Works for Women.

Together with its cadre of volunteers, RBW demolished houses to prepare for new construction; repaired and replaced ceilings, walls and floors; installed full kitchens and bathrooms; and improved drainage and foundations. RBW provided connections to resources, helped with FEMA appeals, assisted in locating temporary housing and offered construction consultations and financial assistance. Volunteers helped organize furniture donations, cleaned homes and helped move families. All totaled, including time spent doing general cleanup in the community, RBW organized over fourteen thousand hours of volunteer labor.

A celebration for people who received support, volunteers and community members was held on January 26, 2013, at Crossett Brook Middle School. Everyone was treated to a free lasagna dinner, and certificates of appreciation recognizing their incredible contributions were issued to volunteers.

5

TROPICAL STORM IRENE

Day One of the Recovery

Rebecca Ellis

As a former chair of the Waterbury Select Board, I am frequently asked what made Waterbury's recovery from Tropical Storm Irene so successful. I like to think that the actions taken by the Select Board and Trustees on the day after the flooding, Monday, August 29, 2011, contain the essential elements of the answer to that question. Throughout the response and recovery process, the Select Board and Trustees' efforts were marked by decisive leadership, concern for public health, organizational vision and robust communications. Those traits were evident from the start.

On the morning of August 29, 2011, I woke up early to drive into Waterbury village. The sun was rising, the waters were receding toward the banks of the river and a glorious day was emerging. Like many people, I had no idea the amount of work that lay ahead. I saw my friend and fellow Select Board member Pam Clapp, who said she had stopped by her house on Randall Street. She remarked that the refrigerator had tipped over and water was still in the house, but she did not think there was much damage. Little did we know that it would be months before she could return home.

Later that morning, municipal manager Bill Shepeluk called me and advised me to call an emergency meeting of the Select Board. The Select Board and Trustees met jointly in the late afternoon, along with municipal staff and some core volunteers. I remain deeply indebted to the Select Board that was in place at that time: Bob Butler, John Grenier, Karen Miller, Pam

A local mail carrier continues with business as usual, surrounded by the ongoing cleanup on Randall Street. *Courtesy of Gordon Miller.*

Clapp and myself. Together we put in many, many hours to organize and support the efforts to rebuild Waterbury.

The Select Board made three critical decisions on day one, decisions that in tone and substance guided Waterbury's entire response for the next eighteen months. First, after some debate and deliberation, the Board opted to provide and pay for trash and debris removal. This decision was not made lightly, since we knew the price tag might be expensive, but we concluded that the risk to public health caused by mountains of trash piled outside people's houses was worth whatever the cost might be. The choice to provide free trash removal had unanticipated and positive long-term effects in Waterbury: the public saw firsthand that the town government was responding decisively and tangibly to the crisis. This buoyed spirits and provided hope to those whose lives were devastated by the disaster.

Second, the Select Board organized a labor swap to take place the next morning, and for the five consecutive days following, in the back parking lot of the Thatcher Brook Primary School. Over 1,300 people came to Waterbury over the next week, from all over the state and country, to help muck out people's homes. Early on, the Select Board learned the

Above: Randall Street was one of the hardest-hit areas in Waterbury. *Courtesy of Gordon Miller.*

Left: Neighbors, friends and volunteers worked together to help and comfort one another during the cleanup process. *Courtesy of Gordon Miller.*

A sign hanging next to the train bridge on North Main Street in Waterbury expressing love for the Waterbury community after Tropical Storm Irene. *Courtesy of Gordon Miller.*

importance of identifying needs and matching them with offers of help, ensuring that contributions were helpful to residents and meaningful to volunteers. This lesson was carried on in the work of ReBuild Waterbury and ultimately the twenty-two projects that made up Waterbury's Long-Term Recovery Plan.

Third, before adjourning on August 29, the Select Board drafted a flyer and organized its distribution to all Waterbury residents whose homes were flooded, to notify them of the trash removal service and the next day's labor swap. The flyer ultimately became a daily newsletter, led by Lisa Scagliotti, who volunteered her wonderful editorial skills and cheery goodwill to get the word out. Good communications and solid information were thus an essential element and a hallmark of Waterbury's recovery effort from the beginning.

The Select Board's decisive actions taken on August 29, 2011—whether by sheer good luck or some innate wisdom—led to a cascade of volunteerism and collaboration and positivity, which in my mind is what made all the difference and kept us Waterbury Strong.

6

THE VERMONT STATE HOSPITAL

Keith Goslant

The Vermont State Hospital (VSH) had withstood both the good and the bad for over a century. Its core buildings were constructed in 1890 in response to overcrowding at the existing psychiatric facility in Brattleboro. At that time, it was known as the Vermont State Asylum for the Insane, a name still used by some federal agencies, such as the Social Security Administration.

During its history, VSH outlasted floods, hurricanes, fires, falling trees, blizzards, earthquakes, changes in leadership, stigma, fear and the unfavorable critiques of inspectors…and inspectors…and inspectors.

It had been held up as a shining standard of care and then later called antiquated and out of touch. During the early 2000s, VSH was decertified by the Joint Commission on Accreditation of Healthcare Organizations (JCAHO), the federal agency charged with inspection and certification. Due to this decertification, VSH was dependent on appropriations from the Vermont legislature for its operating expenses, inclusive of staff salaries. Despite decertification and limited funding, VSH remained committed to meeting the needs of the patients in its care. Each patient had a treatment team and access to ongoing support services, such as individual and group counseling, psychotherapeutic medications, therapeutic rehabilitation services, religious services and staff-supervised activities.

By 2000, the inpatient population had been held at a maximum capacity of 54. This was a dramatic change from the inpatient census during the height of institutionalization, when it reached 1,728. The buildings that constituted VSH had also decreased from the entire campus at 103 South Main Street to merely three or four buildings. The rest of the buildings had been converted for use by other state agencies, including the Department of Mental Health, which was responsible for oversight of VSH. The Vermont legislature continued to review the role of VSH in an overall system of care. There were changes in statutes regulating involuntary psychiatric treatment, reviews of VSH functions and frequent calls for the closure of VSH. Somehow, through it all, VSH always remained intact. Then came the floods of Tropical Storm Irene, and VSH would never be the same.

However, VSH was truly a family, with the challenges all families must face, a family of staff, patients, supporters and critics. Some stayed longer than others, but they have all remained in VSH's memories. Vermont had already endured numerous springtime floods. VSH had thus far always remained on high and dry ground. The impending storm Irene had already been declared a hurricane, later to be downgraded to tropical storm, and the warning was for high winds and flash flooding. VSH prepared as it always had, purchasing and distributing additional batteries and flashlights, checking that all two-way radios were charged and fully operational, moving fleet vehicles to designated parking lots and reviewing call and evacuation protocols. Then the storm hit.

Admission and supervisory staff watched as the floodwaters began to rise, continued to rise and then rose higher than any other Vermont spring flood. When the water started backing up from the culverts, the admission staff notified nursing supervisory staff and moved to higher ground. Soon after, water breached the road, then the parking lots, knocked out the emergency generators and began to encroach on the admission area. Supervisory staff ordered the evacuation of the Brooks Rehab unit to the first-floor Therapeutic Recovery Services area. Patients, charts, mattresses and staff were moved quickly and efficiently. As one staff was leaving the unit, they turned to see the floodwaters coming through the unit windows.

Throughout the night, staff and patients remained close to units that were without electricity, waiting to see what dawn would bring, all the while watching for signs of rising floodwaters, which might prompt the evacuation of the entire Brooks building to the old VSH gymnasium. Building and Ground Services (BGS) navigated flooding tunnels to remove computer servers to higher ground. Several fleet vehicles were lost in parking lots now under several feet of water. From the official reports, at the peak of the storm, the lower levels of VSH were submerged beneath six and a half feet of water, and similar levels were documented at the Osgood Building and other places throughout Waterbury. As dawn finally broke, it became clear that VSH had sustained significant damage.

It would be days before the full extent of the damage would be known; however, the task of assessing immediate needs began immediately. It was clear VSH could not function as a hospital; there was no electricity, water or food service. The lower levels of the hospital were wet, coated with mud, and everything in the flood's path destroyed or displaced. What VSH did have was dedicated and compassionate staff who put patient welfare first.

Throughout the morning, staff made calls to find available bed space in other Vermont psychiatric facilities. Transportation was arranged using a combination of Vermont sheriffs, vehicles on loan from public transportation agencies and VSH staff. The VSH staff was assigned to accompany all patients; there would be a familiar face regardless of where a patient was transferred. Some of the staff members accompanying VSH patients did so knowing the staff member's home had also been in the flood zone and was most likely damaged or destroyed. Food was ordered and delivered; some was donated by businesses such as McDonald's and some paid for by FEMA. Pallets of bottled water were delivered, stacked in hallways and sent to the individual units. Despite the uncertainty of the situation, people approached it in a calm and thoughtful manner, both staff and patients alike. At that time, it was believed the evacuation of VSH would only be temporary. The expectation was VSH would be restored, and the process of transferring patients back would take approximately six weeks. This was not to happen.

During this time, there was a first look at the extent of the damage. Brooks Rehab could not be repopulated. VSH lost the entire medical records, admission, patient benefits, switchboard, facilities management and operations offices. Except for patients' personal belongings and a few personal staff items, everything in these areas would end up in the shredder or a dumpster; even the antique safe was waterlogged. The decision was made: VSH would not reopen.

It had long been the goal of previous administrations to close VSH and replace it with an enhanced community-based system of care and a new state-of-the-art in-patient facility. With the unexpected closure, this now became a true possibility.

VSH has had its share of good-byes. There was a prescribed process: If a client, your social worker or doctor told you that it was time to make discharge plans, you could say goodbye, call your family; you made a visit to your new

Demolition of the Vermont State Hospital Admissions Office after Tropical Storm Irene. *Courtesy of Gordon Miller.*

placement; and you finally signed your aftercare form and walked out the door with family or staff who would accompany you to your destination.

If staff, notice was given with the supervisor's acceptance and a farewell party planned; people would cook, a card was circulated, flowers were arranged, collections were taken and colleagues offered well wishes.

VSH had a means to honor those who had died, former or current, client or staff, with a memorial service held on the unit or in the chapel with time for remembrances and a time for silence. Tropical Storm Irene was not the way we were supposed to say good-bye.

Because there is a morning after, there is more to the story. Following the closure of VSH, the Vermont legislature initiated a comprehensive review of Vermont's system of care for psychiatric services. Based on testimony from providers, advocates, consumers and administrators, the legislature approved funding for the creation of a twenty-five-bed state-of-the-art in-patient facility. The facility would continue to be state run, with the Department of Mental Health providing oversight. After reviewing all options, it was decided the location would be in Berlin adjacent to the Central VT Medical Center. Construction occurred on an aggressive schedule, and the new Vermont Psychiatric Care Hospital (VPCH) was opened on July 1, 2014, and at capacity by that August. In 2015, VPCH received national and international architectural awards for mental health and interior design.

In addition to VPCH, the Vermont system of care currently includes psychiatric/mental health units at the Brattleboro Retreat, UVM Medical Center, Rutland Regional Medical Center, Windham Center and Central VT Medical Center.

7

WATERBURY STATE OFFICE COMPLEX

Engineering Ventures

On August 28–29, 2011, Tropical Storm Irene rained down three to five inches throughout the state of Vermont, with some areas receiving as much as seven inches of rain. The result was massive flooding and devastation of a magnitude not seen since the great flood of 1927. One of the hardest hit areas was the Waterbury Vermont State Campus, where more than twenty buildings were flooded and roughly 1,500 state workers were displaced.

As the floodwaters receded, the State of Vermont and Town of Waterbury immediately began work with FEMA and a team of consultants that evaluated several options, including relocating state offices to a greenfield site in Waterbury or elsewhere, the repair and return to the Waterbury State Office Complex or a partial reuse/restoration and new construction at the Waterbury State Office Complex. The state opted for the partial reuse/restoration and new construction at the Waterbury State Office Complex, which set the stage for several budget, schedule, permitting and engineering challenges.

The main challenge was that much of the Waterbury State Office Campus is located in the one-hundred-year floodplain. The original historic core of the campus, built in the late 1800s as the State Hospital, is situated on the edge of the one-hundred-year floodplain, with the ground floor well below the one-hundred-year flood elevation and the first floor just above the five-hundred-year flood elevation. Since the 1927 flood, the campus had expanded behind the historic core, into the one-hundred-year floodplain. The solution was to deconstruct the twenty-plus badly

Renovation of the Waterbury State Complex after Tropical Storm Irene. The Vermont State Hospital turret structures were maintained. *Courtesy of Gordon Miller.*

damaged and outdated buildings in the floodplain, fill the ground-floor level of the historic core and restore it to its former glory and build a new office building and central plant behind the historic core, all above the five-hundred-year flood elevation.

Through the Vermont Act 250 Land Use Permit process, deconstruction of the twenty-plus buildings (located within a campus on the historic register) was permitted on the condition of restoration of the original historic core buildings. That effort included reintroduction of the historic porte-cochere, cupolas and other features, as well as opening the interior spaces, all of which required bringing the 125-plus-year-old buildings up to current structural code. In addition, the first-floor framing was removed, and the ground-level basement spaces were filled to get no open or occupied spaces below the 500-year flood elevation.

Because the settlement of the historic structure on the floodplain soils was a concern, the ground-floor fill was a combination of lightweight controlled low-strength material (CLSM) fill that was sandwiched between steel fiber–reinforced structural concrete layers. The innovative assembly functions as a mat foundation to distribute building and fill loads to resist excessive settlements; because the CLSM weighs less than water, hydrostatic uplift pressures during future flooding events. This design, called ingenious by the project contractor and steel fiber supplier, saved time by reducing extensive conventional reinforcing placement with steel fibers as it balanced soil pressures and buoyancy.

In addition, a new office building to house the majority of returning State Agency of Human Services employees and a new central plant to power and heat the campus were built. These buildings were also built above the five-hundred-year flood elevation, requiring fill of up to nine feet above existing grade in some cases. The building structure uses a so-called special moment frame. In addition to providing lateral force resistance for the structure, it also functions to enhance structural durability for perimeter column loss in a catastrophic flood event from washout or floating collision. This fill in the floodplain required careful design and coordination across consultant team members and state agencies to remove past fill and structures (including a dormant wastewater treatment plant) from the floodplain to evaluate and ensure that the Winooski River flood elevation would have no rise. In addition, a stormwater treatment system and new flood-proofed utility infrastructure for the campus were installed.

The entire project was authorized by the Vermont legislature, which dictated a budget and schedule that could not be changed. A large team of consultants, contractors and Vermont State Buildings and General Services staff worked to see the project concept become reality, on budget and on time with substantial occupancy of the Campus by Agency of Human Services staff in December 2015, a bit more than four years after Irene.

The project has received the ACEC Vermont Grand Award for Special Projects as well as a Preservation Trust of Vermont Award for Outstanding Work in preserving Vermont's Architecture.

Interior courtyard of the renovated Waterbury State Complex. *Courtesy of Gordon Miller.*

BIBLIOGRAPHY

Fallows, James. "Eleven Signs a City Will Succeed." *The Atlantic*, March 2016. https://www.theatlantic.com/magazine/archive/2016/03/eleven-signs-a-city-will-succeed/426885/.

Town of Waterbury. *Annual Report for the Year Ending December 31, 2020.* https://www.waterburyvt.com/fileadmin/files/Town_clerk_files/Waterbury_Annual_Report_2020.pdf?e6e9332e6343e72b2d80477ad465dbd3d24f99db.

Waterbury Record. "Waterbury Record Publishes Its Last Issue." March 26, 2020.

"Waterbury State Office Complex, Waterbury, VT." Engineering Ventures. Accessed August 4, 2021. https://www.engineeringventures.com/portfolio/waterbury-state-office-complex-waterbury-vt/.

Wuthnow, Robert. *Small-Town America: Finding Community, Shaping the Future.* Princeton, NJ: Princeton University Press, 2013.